WHY IS THERE SUFFERING?

Bethany Sollereder has written a hospitable book, with a light touch. Although an admirably well-informed guide, she allows the visitor to wander at will through many mansions housing one of the most difficult problems to confront thoughtful humanity. Enter, and enjoy finding your own route forward.

Diarmaid MacCulloch, professor emeritus of the history of the church, University of Oxford

Many Christians find themselves "stuck" when it comes to that most profound of questions: accounting for the goodness of God and the existence of suffering. In this highly readable book, Bethany Sollereder offers a lifeline. The reader makes choices after each short chapter about the most helpful next step, and the book constitutes a personalised journey of "reappraisal" of one's beliefs about human and divine agency. Sollereder leads us skilfully through key issues of providence, evil, suffering, divine intervention, and judgment with elegant and accessible prose, and with frequent references to familiar stories and sources. Instead of shutting down debate by attempting to produce a single theological explanation, Sollereder offers a refreshing openness that encourages the pilgrim reader to grow in understanding and in faith. This book will excite and encourage those who are not satisfied with trite answers, and I would recommend it to first-year theology students as well as interested church members.

Sally Nelson, dean of Baptist formation, St Hild College, Yorkshire, and hub tutor for Northern Baptist College

The problem of suffering has been an eternal riddle that has left people puzzled and perplexed for centuries. What I love about this book is its approach to this riddle. It is truly an expedition, and the author knows the terrain inside and out. It reads like a field journal written by a deeply informed guide. If you are looking for an excellent book about *how* to think about this problem, you need look no further. You have found it.

James Bryan Smith, author of *The Good and Beautiful God*

Bethany Sollereder has combined her considerable learning with her passion for theological adventure to produce a book that will help, delight, and provoke many readers. Accessibly written, it will stimulate church study-group discussions, and it also will provide solace for many Christians who have thought some of these thoughts but not known how to connect them up. This is a highly original approach to introducing laypeople to theological reasoning, and I recommend it thoroughly.

Christopher Southgate, professor of Christian theodicy, University of Exeter

Bethany Sollereder is one of the leading scholars within the ongoing debates around the nature of theodicy and how best we should respond to the problem of evil. In this creative and deeply thoughtful book, she presents us with a new, challenging, and deeply promising approach to how best to think about theodicy. This book will not only make an excellent contribution to the field but will also move us on in important directions.

John Swinton, chair in divinity and religious studies, University of Aberdeen, author of *Raging with Compassion: Pastoral Responses to the Problem of Evil*

FOREWORD BY ALISTER E. McGRATH

WHY IS THERE SUFFERING?

Pick Your Own Theological Expedition

BETHANY N. SOLLEREDER

ZONDERVAN REFLECTIVE

Why Is There Suffering?

Requests for information should be addressed to:
Zondervan, *3900 Sparks Dr. SE, Grand Rapids, Michigan 49546*

Zondervan titles may be purchased in bulk for educational, business, fundraising, or sales promotional use. For information, please email SpecialMarkets@Zondervan.com.

ISBN 978-0-310-10902-0 (softcover)
ISBN 978-0-310-13260-8 (audio)
ISBN 978-0-310-10903-7 (ebook)

Cover design: Brock Book Design Co., Charles Brock
Cover photo: © fran_kie / Shutterstock
Interior design: Denise Froehlich

Printed in the United States of America

---

21 22 23 24 25 /LSCH/ 10 9 8 7 6 5 4 3 2 1

For Mom and Dad,
who always let me choose my own paths,
no matter how perilous

I'll tell you a secret:
The firebrand begins
as a sapling.
If you mark her long
journey to flame, watch for
the spark near the roots.
Years later when she
explodes in light, you won't so much
as cock an eyebrow.

—Haley Hodges Schmid

The First Decision

Let's begin with a decision:

I start at the beginning. (Turn to the foreword by Alister McGrath on p. xi.)

I like hearing the rationale of a book. (Turn to the introduction on p. xv.)

I hate instructions and preamble. On with the adventure! (Turn to p. 1 [ch. 1].)

I don't like adventure into the unknown. Is there a map somewhere? (Turn to p. 158.)

I'm already lost! I need to see a good old-fashioned table of contents. (Turn to p. 179.)

Who was involved with this? Take me to the acknowledgments. (Turn to p. 155.)

Foreword

How do we make sense of the presence of evil and suffering in the world? Our answers to this question are often described as *theodicies*, meaning ways of safeguarding God's goodness and integrity in the face of a suffering world. It is a question that can be traced back to the Old Testament and has never ceased to engage thoughtful minds through the ages. Might it be possible to imagine a world in which there was no suffering? No fall? No evil? In the past, two main approaches have been used. Some offer an imaginative exploration of the question, similar to what we find in C. S. Lewis's masterpiece *Perelandra*. Might it be possible for someone from earth to prevent the fall happening somewhere else? How could the fall be avoided? And what would history look like if it never took place? We cannot answer these questions. Lewis, however, helps us imagine what might have happened, as a way of allowing us to appreciate the complexities of living in our own fallen world.

The second approach is that of philosophers of religion, who offer us occasionally elegant and generally erudite reflections on how we can understand the existence of evil in terms of the interplay of human freedom and divine goodness. Many have written on this important issue, often offering us subtle variations on the approaches we find in writers such as Augustine of Hippo. Eminent writers like Richard Swinburne and Alvin Plantinga have penned insightful ways of holding together God's goodness and the reality of suffering. Leading academic presses have produced large companion volumes to the "problem of evil," laying out and assessing the main approaches, leaving us to figure out which seems the most persuasive and inviting us to reflect on the assumptions we bring to this discussion. Should we *really* be disturbed by the existence of suffering in our world? And is this *really* a defeater for belief in God?

These two approaches have many strengths. But there is a third, represented by Bethany Sollereder, a postdoctoral research fellow at Oxford University, who has researched various ways of making sense of suffering within the world, especially in light of Darwinian theories of evolution. Although she brings the fruit of her research to bear on this book, Bethany avoids the density and detail that make so many discussions of this question difficult to follow. Bethany's approach is to invite us to build our own theodicies and reflect on how persuasive we find them. As we think through these questions, we must make choices about which path to follow based on the assumptions that shape our ideas.

How does this book work? Bethany helps us to explore options through this intellectual maze by pointing out the various pathways available, inviting us to explore them in her company, and asking what we make of them. If we find that a pathway takes us to a dark place, we simply retrace our steps, choose a different pathway, and see how that works out. It's a guided tour of options, intended to help readers explore them with a courteous and informed guide who accompanies them as they wander and reflect.

Yes, it's a simple approach, but it helps us appreciate that our thinking about the presence of suffering in the world is shaped by the assumptions we bring to our reflections. What if there are better ways of thinking that we haven't explored yet? It's the kind of approach a scientist would adopt: identify the various intellectual options and see which makes most sense of the evidence. In the case of theodicy, this evidence is located in the biblical witness to the character of God and the nature of humanity, as well as our own experience of suffering in the world around us. Bethany invites us to explore those options and work out what we think works best—and why.

Yet Bethany's approach does more than help Christians clarify their own thinking on this matter. She helps us understand how others think. For example, Christians who are confronted with the issue of suffering might feel the problem arises from believing that God loves us and is perfectly good. But what happens if there is no God? Do atheists get an easier ride? Bethany invites us to explore the atheist pathway and discover where it leads.

I hope you enjoy this intellectual ride and that it helps you think through the challenges of living in a world of pain, suffering, and evil. We may not be able to solve these intellectual riddles as neatly as we would like, but we can certainly find a way to live with them.

Alister McGrath
Andreas Idreos Professor of Science and Religion
University of Oxford

Turn to the next page.

Introduction

You have chosen to read the rationale for this book.

Let me begin with a confession: I don't know why you picked up this book.

I do not know whether watching the evening news has raised questions about the goodness of God in light of daily global tragedies or whether some hidden hurt that only you know of has made you wonder about the God you've loved. Maybe you have never believed in God, yet you find yourself resenting God all the same. Because I don't know those things, it would be arrogant for me to think I have better explanations for your pain than you do. I know neither the circumstances of your pain nor the solutions to it. In this book, I will not try to provide those answers.

Instead, this book is designed to help you explore theological options. Academics have hammered out many ideas about suffering in the dark corners of musty libraries over the years, and this book brings them out into the light of day.

This book is not meant to be read like a traditional book from front to back. Indeed, if you try to read it that way, you will likely end up highly disoriented, and nothing will make sense. Instead, this book is meant to be read along certain paths. At the end of each chapter, you will be asked to make choices about God, the world, and evil. Each choice you make will direct you to a certain page number, and you should flip there directly, skipping over any intervening pages.

Each choice will lead you through theological landscapes that follow on from earlier choices. You are in control of the decisions you make; you decide which explanations work. You can always go back and see what would change if you had made a different choice. Sometimes you may find that more than one answer seems like the right answer. There can be more than one reason for suffering, and different explanations can offer depth and perspective on a situation. Not every choice is an either/or, so feel free to mix and match the paths.

Some people will be uncomfortable with the idea of picking their own theology. Don't we simply accept God's revelation? Isn't it a problem to think we can decide what God is like? I felt this way for a long time. But eventually I realized that God and suffering are great mysteries.[1] Even the best minds cannot get to the bottom of them, so we do the best we can. We are like detectives trying to piece together a coherent picture from a confounding number of hints and whispers.

The truth is that theologians don't describe what God is really like; we only work with models of God. Like a model car or train, our models of God are laughably smaller and simpler than the real thing.

Knowing this, we hold our theological positions with open hands. We understand the limited sight we possess and the difficulty of speaking well about God. Anytime we make theological decisions, we highlight certain parts of what we think is important

---

1. A mystery is not something that can never be known. Rather, the more you know about a mystery, the more you realize you've only scratched the surface of what there is to know. Every time you answer one question, three more appear. In this sense, much of the world is mysterious, from God right down to the nature of physical matter.

about God, while obscuring others. Every time we say, "God is like *this*," we must then say, "but not entirely. Actually, God is like *that* too." Having lots of models of God ensures we remember that we are, after all, only working with models.

This book gives various options, but not all of them agree with each other. I deeply disagree with some of the paths I've written. Yet each is an example of how real people have chosen to understand God and suffering. Each path is a model someone has used.

Exploring other people's views about God, even if we don't agree with them, helps us see some of the strengths and shortfalls of our own position. So I invite you into the theological choices in this book with a sense of play. I have no answers or agenda to change your mind. I simply hope to provide a different set of ideas than you may have already encountered. Making meaning of your experience in light of these positions is still work you will have to do. I cannot do it for you, nor will I tell you what to think.

You may find that certain pathways resonate with your experience in a way you did not expect. You may find that a path you were sure was the best now seems weaker than you initially thought. That's okay. Try a new path and see what happens. You can always go back to the former path if you need to. In fact, if you come to a point where you can't decide which path to take because too many seem right, leave a bookmark and come back to it later.

Is there any truth at the bottom of the positions? As a confessing Christian, I certainly think some paths are closer to the truth than others. But I am also aware that God is bigger than our theologies. Sometimes our different descriptions of God may seem incompatible, but each points to a certain kind of truth. The optical illusion below is based on a drawing originally published in 1892 in the magazine *Fliegende Blätter* by an anonymous illustrator and later popularized by psychologist Joseph Jastrow.

Is it a duck? Is it a rabbit? Both options are good descriptions, depending on how you look at it. In reality, we are looking at a series of lines and dots on a page, but we recognize them as a duck or a rabbit. Someone seeing only the duck could get quite cross at the person who sees only the rabbit. A rabbit is not a duck! It is incompatible to say a rabbit could be a duck. And that person would be right. But that person would be wrong too. Imagine this pattern of lines as an ear instead of a beak and—*voilà*!—a rabbit emerges. Obviously, both are truer than saying the image looks like an elephant. Having two possible perspectives doesn't mean anything goes.

I don't know how often our descriptions of God are like the rabbit-duck illusion. When one set of people says God is eternal, unchanging, and unaffected, I assume they are telling the truth about what they have discovered about God. When another group says they feel God weeping with them in their sorrows—that God is closer, more personal, and more intimate than a lover—I listen to that too. I assume that all the positions, even the ones I don't agree with or the ones that are incompatible with each other, tell us something about God, the world, and our own human nature. (People who claim the picture is an elephant may only be telling us they need new glasses—but that is a useful truth too!)

I have no key, no viewpoint, that unlocks the singular truth embedded in these multiple experiences of God. Instead, I am simply representing them as well as I can. I hope you will find them useful as you figure out what makes sense to you. This is a guidebook, or a map. I can lay out the intellectual terrain, point out highlights, show the major routes and some of the smaller tracks.

But it is up to you to decide which paths to take. I hope that it will be a lighthearted adventure, despite the heavy topic. In order to keep a light tone, with only one exception, you will not find graphic illustrations of suffering in this book. I assume that if you are reading this book, you already know about suffering. My hope is that this little introduction will help you work out what kind of approaches you will find most helpful.

Many others have written much longer, more complete explorations of these potential answers. If you want to read more about any position described in the pages that follow, you will find a bibliography at the end of the book organized by chapter. In those books you will find all the things you will not find here: the history behind each position, who developed the approach, the formal logic, the technical words, the nuanced arguments over which position is best. I encourage you to dig deeper into the areas that interest you—this book is only a beginning.

I think that's all the introduction needed for now. The bags are packed, the coats are on, the guidebook is in hand, and we have some snacks for the road (I like apples and cheese for walking, but what you bring is up to you). Unlike Bilbo Baggins, we've even remembered our handkerchiefs. Are we all ready? Then let's go!

Turn to p. 1 [ch. 1].

What Is God Like?

Your journey begins as you set out from home, the road running before you smooth and straight. You walk for some time, recalling the experiences that call into question the deep realities of life. Up ahead, you can see the road branching three different ways.

The heart of the theological problem with suffering stems from God being both powerful and loving. If God is perfectly powerful, then God should be able to prevent suffering. If God is perfectly loving, God should want to prevent suffering. The Christian tradition describes God as almighty and perfectly loving, yet we still suffer.

We don't just suffer a little bit, either. For all its goodness and beauty, this is a tearstained existence. I don't need to recount the horrors that exist in our world because you already know many of them. You've read about them, watched them, and experienced them yourself. Even without the horrors we see on television, there is enough trouble in our day-to-day lives to make us wonder what God is up to and how God could allow the evils we experience.

I remember once sitting in church when despair was sitting heavy on me and trying to sing along to the chorus, "You are so good, so good, so good to me." The words felt hollow. God's goodness certainly did not seem evident to me. Is God really good? It is an appropriate question to ask at the beginning of our adventure, and it is one many have asked as they contemplated suffering in the world.

There are three major approaches we could take to that question. First, there is the possibility that God *is* perfectly good. More than just good—God is love. God is the source of all life, and God's love is the secret wellspring of all that is. The world is not just a creative project but is the offspring of God's overflowing love. God's perfect will of good for the world may be impeded by various factors (we will talk about those later), but God essentially desires the well-being of the world and all that is in it. The world is not perfect for one of two reasons: either God has been opposed by some other being (like Satan), or created beings themselves reject God's plan.

Second, we might think God is not good or loving. Perhaps good and evil run through God equally, like the yin and yang concept of Chinese philosophy. Or, like the Force from *Star Wars*, God only seeks to keep balance in the universe. Perhaps God is entirely neutral—neither good nor evil in essence. God is, on this reading, only the empowering source of life. Maybe God is simply not interested in this world or its troubles; God created the world and set the heavenly spheres spinning, but now God is off somewhere doing other things. Perhaps God is busy creating new universes, and our troubles do not reach the divine attention. Whatever the reason, evil exists because God does not oppose it or doesn't care.

The third option is that God simply does not exist. Therefore, the world is one that is indifferent to suffering because there is no loving or caring being to look out for us. There is not even a neutral being to ignore us. We simply *are* in this vast, beautiful, and terrifying cosmos, inhabiting a pale blue dot of a planet.

There is the agnostic approach, too—that we don't know what

God is like or if God exists. I won't include that as an option because it cannot go beyond its initial statement of "there is not sufficient evidence to decide." (I've only included options where people *make* claims about reality.) But an open-minded agnostic could read all the paths with some benefit, because being better informed about the options is never a bad thing. In other areas where there is not enough evidence to make a final decision—like whether gravity is quantum or classical—the lack of deciding evidence does not make being well-informed a less noble pursuit.

It's time to decide: What do you believe God is like?

God is perfectly good and loves us. (Turn to p. 4 [ch. 2].)

God exists but doesn't love us. (Turn to p. 36 [ch. 13].)

God does not exist. (Turn to p. 41 [ch. 15].)

CHAPTER 2

God Is Love

You take the road that veers off to the left, toward distant mountains. To your right, open plains show the wide, bright sky. Farther right, almost behind you, you can see the road rise up a hill, and at the top you see a bridge across a hidden canyon.

"God is love," writes John in his letter (1 John 4:8). Christians look primarily to the Bible to understand what God is like, and the Bible describes God as full of unfailing love. In one way, that tells you all you need to know about God. Love captures all that is truly good, worthy, and right in the world. In another way, that might tell you very little. After all, love can mean all sorts of things. You can love a friend, but you can also love a hamburger. Your "love" for your hamburger will lead to you eating it, but hopefully that is not true of your friend!

Generally, when we say God is love—that God loves us—we mean that God wants the best for us. God wants things to go well with us. We could even add that God wants to be in a relationship with us, since knowing God is part of what is best for us.

So far so good.

But when we look around at the world, it doesn't seem like what is best for us actually happens. We certainly don't see a world where all people are in a loving relationship with God or with each other. Quite the contrary. So what has gone wrong?

There are four possible choices about God at this point.

First, you can say that God is indeed all-powerful and all-knowing, but there is confusion somewhere else in the picture. Maybe God has a plan to use evil for good. Maybe the reason God allows evil is simply too hard for us to understand, and our job is merely to hold on in faith. Whatever the case, the existence of evil does not indicate that something has gone wrong in God's plan. All power and all knowledge sit with God eternally.

Second, you can say that, because God loves us, God gives us the freedom to choose actions that don't lead to the best outcome for ourselves or others. We can even refuse relationship with God if we so choose. Love gives freedom, even when it hurts. Our freedom can disrupt God's good plans for us.

Third, you can believe that God's power is limited for some other reason. Maybe God isn't all-powerful in the first place. God wants good to happen but doesn't have the ability to bring about the best outcomes. Maybe God has an opponent (like Satan) who gets in the way and messes things up. Or perhaps it is not in God's nature to coerce or control at all. God's power is not the kind that controls stuff and causes things to happen; rather it empowers and allows others to cause things to happen.

Finally, there is the possibility that God doesn't know the future. While traditional Christianity has usually said something like "God sees everything, past, present, and future," what if, in order to have real relationship with people, God has given up that eternal vantage point? Just as Jesus became a human with all a human's limitations, so God chose to experience time with us and therefore creates the future with us. When bad things happen, they are not part of God's plan, but God will *turn them into* part of the plan by the end of time. Like Rumpelstiltskin, God can spin gold out of straw, so not knowing or planning the future is of little importance. It is more important to God that there is real give-and-take, real response in relationship with us.

The paths lie before you. Which way will you choose?

God is all-powerful and all-knowing, so either there is a plan or suffering is a mystery. (Turn to p. 7 [ch. 3].)

We have the freedom to disrupt God's plan. (Turn to p. 17 [ch. 7].)

God's power is limited. (Turn to p. 20 [ch. 8].)

God does not know the future. (Turn to p. 24 [ch. 9].)

CHAPTER 3

God Is All-Powerful and All-Knowing

You've taken the path toward the high mountains, approaching the foothills. The mountains seem to call, enchanting and mysterious, wild and free, drawing you forward into the unknown. As you walk toward them, you notice a broad, smooth road extending to your right. It is the first paved surface you have seen. You stand at the beginning of the road, but the mountains still call. You pause to consider the next path.

God is all-powerful and all-knowing. God sees the end from the beginning, standing outside time and space. God knows exactly what you will do tomorrow in just the same way that God knows what you did yesterday.

In addition, God is all-powerful. Nothing happens without God's express permission. God inspires every good action. When bad happens, it is not because things are outside of God's control.

On one hand, this can be comforting. It means you can give up trying to control situations. You can rest in the knowledge that "underneath are the everlasting arms" (Deut 33:27). No matter how bad things get, God has things under control and knows exactly how they are going to turn out. You may feel out of control, but the universe never is.

On the other hand, it raises some difficult questions. If God is all-powerful—if the world proceeds according to plan—why did God include evil and suffering in the first place? If God is in control, even over our free choices and any demonic powers, why didn't God create in a way that evil couldn't happen? Or why not create in a way that there is far less evil? We could still have free choice if our choices had far less serious consequences.

If God is all-powerful and all-knowing, the question still begs to be asked: "Why is there evil?"

There are two possibilities. The first is that everything is a mystery. We can come up with a thousand possibilities and end in the same place that we started: not knowing. The reason for suffering and evil is God's business alone.

The second option is that God has a plan. Evil is allowed—tolerated—because God is going to turn it into good. In the meantime, all pain and all sorrow are somehow necessary to contribute to the perfection of that ultimate goal. God's plan is like a broad road, a well-paved path, that does not have any surprises.

It is time to decide: If God is all-powerful and all-knowing, how can suffering still exist?

It's a mystery; we can't know why suffering exists.
(Turn to p. 9 [ch. 4].)

God has a plan. (Turn to p. 14 [ch. 6].)

CHAPTER 4

Suffering Is a Mystery

The call of the mountains won you over. You left the broad path and walked into the wild country. After a few hours, you find yourself in the rough and rugged territory of the foothills.

Life is a mystery. God's ways are a mystery. God is the greatest mystery of all. We humans, with our small brains and short lives, are not in a good position to make decisions about the ultimate questions of good and evil or what makes a life worthwhile. Maybe we can see value in life, and only the reasons for evil will ultimately elude us. Either way, we simply can't know enough to come up with any definite answers.

After all, there are far simpler things we can't know. Physicists have improved their understanding of how matter moves through space—enough to send spaceships to the farthest reaches of our solar system. But big, heavy things moving through the vacuum of space represent the simplest kind of motion to calculate. Take a feather and throw it off the roof of a building, and no physicist on earth can tell you where it will land. The uncertainty of the ever-shifting winds combined with the feather's ability to switch direction at the slightest change in pressure means there are too many variables to count.

If we cannot calculate the movement of a feather in the wind, how in the world will we calculate the balance of good and evil or pleasure and suffering in the world? To even attempt this is far too bold. Only the proudest and least reflective would even try.

And only the most insensitive would try to explain the meaning behind the tragedies we hold in our hearts. If we have found some measure of peace with the ways we have been mistreated or with the suffering we have seen, it is only by grace. Maybe those sharp edges in our souls have been dulled by constant contact, like running a finger over a sharp piece of glass until it is smooth, blunted into a simple longing: "Why?" But big words and logical answers do little except miss the point. They leave us feeling even more misunderstood than before.

When we encounter the mystery of suffering, we should not try to explain; we should simply lament, resist, heal, and hold each other through the darkest night.

Is it all, always, ultimately mystery? Is there nothing we can say about how God might draw together history in redemptive ways? Does a vision of hope not help? You arrive at the foot of the first true mountain. The way to the peaks of final mystery lies before you, and yet another path snakes down toward a distant aquamarine river, sparkling in the late afternoon sun. It calls you to the resolution of all things.

It is time to decide: Is there a chance for making meaning of suffering?

Nope, stop trying to make sense of the senseless, and keep climbing. (Turn to p. 12 [ch. 5].)

Suffering is ultimately a mystery, but it is still sometimes helpful and hopeful to think about how God might redeem us. Head toward the river. (Turn to p. 102 [ch. 34].)

CHAPTER 5

Living with Mystery All the Way Down

After a long and difficult climb, you reach the peak of the mountain. You can look out on all the landscape below you: the rivers, plains, moors, fields, and forests. Despite the beauty of the view, you cannot find a pattern in the landscape below. Although there are roads heading in all directions, you realize the territory is wilder and less developed than you thought. You sit to contemplate the vista.

It is human nature to figure things out, to problem solve, to fix. But we must resist that urge. Instead, it is better to sit in silence with suffering. (Even Job's friends were wise—until they opened their mouths.)

Grief is the fracturing of meaning. For someone else to try to apply meaning feels oppressive, like they are slapping a Band-Aid on a wound they don't want to see anymore. Trying to piece answers together yourself also feels impossible. The world has stopped making sense, almost as if everything was translated into an unknown language when you weren't looking.

If this is the case, you don't need a set of instructions; you need someone to trust. Let the Marthas of the world debate with Jesus about the resurrection of the dead. What you need is to see that Jesus weeps with us, to know that he hears your lament.

God has not told us why the world is the way it is, nor why evil and accidents and illness seem to rule the day. But God has promised to be with us. "I will not leave you as orphans; I will come to you" (John 14:18). How is God present? God comes to us through the Holy Spirit and through other people. "Where two or three gather in my name, there am I with them" (Matt 18:20). Through the hands and feet of others, through their embraces and tears, in the community of others who have known tragedy, through the indwelling Spirit, God is present. The compassion we show each other is the only answer to suffering we are likely to have in this life.

God's presence isn't an answer to our cries. God provides no explanation. But God is listening when we lament. God hears us when we protest. Suffering ushers us, somehow, into the greatest mystery of all: living and trusting in the life of God. Our task is simply to learn to live in the mystery and to walk with those who are suffering.

You have reached the end of this path.

You may end here or go back to the last major decision point. (Turn to p. 7 [ch. 3].)

CHAPTER 6

God Has a Plan

You follow the broad, paved path, enjoying the sudden ease of travel and your ability to both walk and watch. On less certain roads, you have to consider carefully where you put each foot, lest you trip on some unseen obstacle, but here you can walk confidently. The beauty of the landscape takes your breath away as you continue on your journey.

God has a plan. In everything, God is sovereign over the events of the world. As Romans 8:28 says, "We know that in all things God works for the good of those who love him, who have been called according to his purpose." That means God intends everything good, but that God also wills all the evil that happens. Why? Because, somehow, those things are for God's greater glory and our greater good.

A glance at the newspapers seems to reveal that to be impossible. God could not possibly will such evil in the world to exist. But God's ways are not our ways. Consider the great, mysterious goodness of the cross.

From one point of view, the crucifixion of Jesus is the most outrageous evil. The perfectly good, perfectly loving Christ is put to death in an agonizing and humiliating way. Yet in Acts 2:23 Peter tells the crowd, "This man was handed over to you by God's deliberate plan and foreknowledge." Why would God plan this? Because it brought about the salvation of the world. Jesus's crucifixion was brought about by evil people desiring what was evil, but God had a different, hidden plan to bring about great good.

In *The Lion, the Witch and the Wardrobe*, Aslan[1] goes willingly to his death at the hands of the White Witch. She does not know about the "deeper magic" that will turn her apparent moment of victory into a resounding defeat. The White Witch willed Aslan's death for one reason, and Aslan willed it for an entirely different reason. He knew it would grant him the power to undo all the evil she had laid down. Aslan knew her evil actions were ultimately self-defeating, that the knife she used to kill him was actually cutting apart the cords she had used to bind the land in slavery. He willed that she should do this freely chosen evil act, even though it meant his own suffering.

Our lives are different, though. We don't willingly go into most of the suffering we encounter. If we had a way to avoid it, we would. Aslan and Jesus both had the choice to undergo their suffering, but we don't get that choice. God chooses that we should undergo suffering in the divine plan for a similar redemption. Why does God choose that we should suffer?

First, it could be because suffering gives us the possibility to mature. Suffering makes us stronger, so God allows us to undergo these things so we will grow or to prepare us for some future trial. Ultimately, suffering will be useful for us.

1. Author C. S. Lewis described Aslan as an answer to the question: "What might Christ become like if there really were a world like Narnia and He chose to be incarnate and die and rise again in that world as he actually has done in ours?" ("Letter to Mrs. Hook, December 29, 1958," in Walter Hooper, *C. S. Lewis: A Companion and Guide* [San Francisco: HarperCollins, 1996], 424–25).

Second, it could be because our suffering is necessary to some other great good. Your brain might direct your feet to walk over painful gravel, not because it is good for your feet but because your body needs to go somewhere down the road. God allows us to undergo terrible experiences, not because we benefit from them but because our suffering serves a wider good.

The broad path forks into two different paths, both smooth and straight. But the weather ahead looks dodgy. Ahead of the first road are dark clouds and heavy rain. The second road disappears into a dense bank of fog.

Which way will you go?

Suffering offers possibilities for our growth.
(Turn to p. 68 [ch. 24].)

God has a bigger picture we can't see.
(Turn to p. 71 [ch. 25].)

CHAPTER 7

Freedom

You head for the open plains and soon find yourself walking amid a wild grass meadow. The tall grass blows in the wind, and you enjoy the feeling of wide possibility.

Freedom is the reason bad things happen. People, or perhaps other agents,[1] use their God-given freedom to harm others. But this leaves us with a puzzle. If God has given real freedom, then that seems to limit God's power or knowledge. God might have the choice to give freedom in the first place, but once God gives real choice to creatures, it is up to them to decide what to do.

There are, of course, different kinds of freedom. You can choose to walk in any direction you like if there are no walls around you, but you cannot choose to fly with your arms. You can choose to switch houses, but you can't choose to switch bodies. Freedom, of whatever type, is always limited. The same is true for God. Once God created the world with free beings, God became limited.

There are four different ways you can think about how those limits apply. The first option is that God is limited in power: God

1. If you think the free will of demons is the problem, you can skip straight there by turning to p. 27 [ch. 10].

gave such radical freedom that even God can't stop evil from happening. God would like evil to stop happening, but an intervention to stop harm would mean stripping away the very gift of freedom God gave in the first place. Some inconsiderate people give gifts and then take them back if they think they are being poorly used, but God is not like that. God will never rip the gift of freedom from the hands of the receiver. God gives for keeps, and when the world was created, it was given the powerful, beautiful, and dangerous gift of choice. Ever after, God has been limited in power.

The second option is that God is limited in knowledge. God can act in the world through miracles and in other ways, yet when God gave free choice, God also gave up the ability to know the exact future. God may know all possibilities of the future, but not which path people will actually choose. God allows an open future in order to allow us freedom. In this case, there are two reasons God doesn't just miracle away all suffering. The first is because God has given freedom and does not wish to take it away (although sometimes God might). The second is because God can work creatively with our bad decisions to redeem them. God not only makes lemonade from lemons but brings life from death and good from evil. *How* that will happen is still an open question, but *that* it will happen is assured.

The third option is that God is all-powerful and knows the exact future, and we still have perfect freedom. This initially seems impossible. How can it work? How can God know all your future actions and yet they can still be freely chosen? There's no perfect explanation, but it might be a bit like how my friends know that, if I walk into an ice-cream shop, I will always choose chocolate ice cream. I have perfect freedom to choose lemon sorbet or mint. But every time I am faced with the choice, I freely choose chocolate because, at bottom, that is what I want the most. God's knowledge of us is so intimate that God knows in every case what we most desire. So, without playing around with our freedom, God can perfectly know our free choices even before we make them. In this case, although God knows the future, God doesn't choose the future; we do. Therefore, even if we accept that God is all-powerful, we still say that God does not *cause* everything. So we end up saying (with the first choice) that God's power does not decide everything that happens.

The final option is that God causes everything, and we have perfect freedom. Surely *that* must be a contradiction! But we see examples of this in certain circumstances. Think of a sheep dog rounding up sheep in a competition. By nature, the dog would have no reason to get sheep to go around several fences and then walk themselves into a pen. The dog only carries out these actions because the shepherd "causes" the dog to want that outcome. Yet the dog acts in perfect physical freedom. The shepherd has not taken control of the dog's legs or intelligence. The dog simply performs in obedience to what the shepherd asks, but the shepherd is the ultimate cause of the dog's actions. In this option, all our actions are like that—we freely choose what we do, but the ultimate cause of our actions is God.

Out of those four options, how do you think human freedom applies limits to God?

God is limited in power. (Turn to p. 20 [ch. 8].)

God is limited in knowledge. (Turn to p. 24 [ch. 9].)

God knows the free choices we will make but does not make the future. (Turn to p. 20 [ch. 8].)

God causes everything, and we have perfect freedom. (Turn to p. 33 [ch. 12].)

CHAPTER 8

God Has Limited Power

As you walk, the land slowly rises. Then a steep ravine opens in front of you, blocking your way. Deep below, a stream winds its way through the small canyon. The walls of the canyon are too steep to climb, but, looking around, you see a rope bridge spanning the chasm. It looks more than a bit questionable as you approach it. You finally conclude that there is no other way across—if you want to continue your journey this way, there is only one way to proceed. You must trust the bridge.

You make your way across and find the bridge more solid than you anticipated, although it sometimes sways alarmingly. On the far side, you see three diverging paths: one heads off left toward a river, one enters a young deciduous wood straight ahead of you, and the last track turns right toward a distant valley. You pause to consider your options.

Most people generally think of God as all-powerful. In fact, that is almost a basic definition of God. But what do we mean by *all-powerful*? Surely it cannot mean that God can do nonsensical things, like make a married bachelor or solve the classic dilemma, "Can God make a rock so big that God cannot lift it?" Some things are impossible because they make no sense. God cannot make a round square because that would contradict the definition of a square.

Other things are not impossible in themselves, but they become impossible once God has chosen to commit to a certain version of reality. For example, if creation involves free agents, those agents must be able to choose evil. If they couldn't choose evil, then they would not be truly free.

Evil in the world comes in many forms. Some people limit the word *evil* to moral wrongs like acts of violence. But others use *evil* to describe natural occurrences as well. Harmful events like earthquakes or cancers are sometimes called "natural evil," though some theologians prefer to call them simply "harms" or "disvalues." So why do these harmful things exist? It comes down to a limit of some sort placed on God's power.

But what is the source of that limit? There are three options for why the world isn't a perfect reflection of God's will. The first is that free will is the answer (you may have arrived here by that path already, but there is more to explore along that path). God doesn't decide what happens in the world; creatures do. Using admittedly metaphorical language, we can include rocks, the sun, and gravity as "creatures" too. The natural processes of the world and the free choices of living creatures create environments where suffering happens. God did not design suffering. Creatures largely made themselves by exercising free will, and that has led to suffering. Once upon a time, a very long time ago, a hungry prehistoric ancestor to the tiger looked at something soft and fluffy and thought, *You know, I could probably eat that.* That long-lost ancestor started a trend that continues today in their feline descendants. The hurricane spins destruction because that is what air in certain configurations freely does. People choose evil because they are given moral freedom to choose good or evil.

There is simply no other way for them to mature; otherwise, they would be mere puppets forever.

However, although God allows creatures significant and harm-causing amounts of freedom, creation is not a total free-for-all. God is constantly acting in various ways to respond to suffering. Investigating those actions is where the river path will lead you.

A second option is that God is limited in power because of evil agents at work in the world. In short, God is at war. Tradition maintains that before the start of time, the greatest of angels rebelled against God. Lucifer and his followers were cast from the glories of heaven. Ever since, they have roamed invisibly through creation, causing mayhem, destruction, and despair. In this option, the answer to the question, "Why is there suffering?" is that the universe is a cosmic battlefield. God doesn't create evil; that is instead the work of an enemy. Our place in the world is like that of Allied soldiers between D-Day and V-Day. After the conquest at Normandy, the outcome of World War II was assured, but the fight still had to be completed. God's power is limited by the devil's opposition, but even though the outcome is assured, the fight still has to be carried out. The battle is straight ahead in the trees.

The last option is that it is impossible for God to act coercively because of God's great love. In the first two choices, God willingly gave free will to humans and demons, but God can and someday will take it away when it comes time to wrap up history and give evil a resounding and final defeat. But in this choice, love itself is deemed to be entirely noncoercive. Since God is love, God can never, ever force events or people toward certain conclusions. Divine power is seen not in God's powerful triumph over other creatures but in God's ability to empower creatures to grow in love and maturity. If they choose not to grow, or to grow in discord and malice instead,

God is limited to persuading them toward the good. God can't stop evil. To explore this further, head for the distant valley.

It is time to decide. Which path of limitation will you take?

God gives free will, which accounts for suffering, and God acts to respond to suffering. (Turn to p. 64 [ch. 23].)

God is at war with Satan. (Turn to p. 27 [ch. 10].)

God can never coerce. (Turn to p. 30 [ch. 11].)

CHAPTER 9

God Does Not Know the Future

Your walk along the road leads you into a set of wheatfields. The heads of the grain are a ripe, golden color, and the fields sway in a light breeze rising from the west. The rippling gold landscape seems sentient, the soft murmuring of the plants whispering secrets to one another. Overhead, an eagle soars in the clear blue sky, patiently circling on the updrafts, seeking this day's sustenance with her keen eyes. There is some evidence of a farmer's cultivation in these fields, some regularity to the rows that your eye can almost catch. Yet there is also a wild and unplanned feel to these fields, as if seed was scattered rather than planted in plowed furrows. You begin to ponder as you walk.

What if God does not know the future? That seems scary. We like ordered plans: straight lines, careful blueprints, reliable investment strategies. We enjoy the idea of God as an architect, carefully planning every aspect of our environment. But what if God were more like an artist? The riotous color and wild diversity of life suggest a *creative* rather than a *rational* approach. The creator of the elephant seal had to have a sense of humor, and the maker of cuttlefish leaves one wondering about the terrible goodness of divine creativity.

In the Bible, we can overhear God negotiating with Moses and with Abraham over the fates of nations and cities. God seems to want to work with people. We can hear God's exasperated cry of longing over his rebellious people in Hosea 11:8: "How can I give you up, Ephraim? . . . How can I treat you like Admah? . . . My heart is changed within me; all my compassion is aroused." God is great *because* God changes.

Does that mean the future sits on shaky foundations? An artistic approach doesn't always yield the most stable or reliable results. Wouldn't it be better to have a divine accountant who makes sure everything is balanced at the end of the day?

Theologian John Sanders imagines God more like a jazz musician than an architect. In jazz, none of the musicians knows quite how the song will go. They work together and improvise off each other. If one makes a mistake, the others can weave the mistake into a new melody.[1]

There are lots of things to like about imagining God as heaven's Ella Fitzgerald.[2] It means the point of creation is in the doing, not in getting to the end. If creation is God's song, it is the performance that matters. In jazz, each moment is a risk, where the artists strive to create beauty and harmony and novelty out of uncertainty. Sometimes they fail. God is working with amateurs, after all, so the song may be full of mistakes.

Trust in God, in this case, is not rooted in God's perfect plan

1. John Sanders, *The God Who Risks: A Theology of Divine Providence* (Downers Grove, IL: IVP Academic, 2009), 245.

2. Ella Fitzgerald is often known as the first lady of song or the queen of jazz. Even if you do not know a lot of jazz, you perhaps know her famous recording with Louis Armstrong of "Let's Call the Whole Thing Off."

or God's ability to control all things at all times. Trust is placed in God's amazing ability to transform even our most discordant mistakes and earsplitting acts into melodies of grace. Our mess-ups are unforced errors, but they can be reconfigured as essential plot points. This story is one of growth and learning. Useless suffering becomes something useful after all, by the grace of God. If humans had made different choices or the alignment of coincidences had happened another way, then God would have found some other resolution, and history would have turned down another path.

The bottom line is that God shares the work of creating with us. Again, think of the biblical story: when God created the world in Genesis 2, God made a garden for people to live in. Later, people used their skills and imagination to create cities. But the place of the redeemed in the book of Revelation at the end of the story is a compromise of both. The New Jerusalem is a garden-city. It is a coming together of divine creativity and human innovation. God takes our inventions and turns them into part of the good story of creation.

Even though freedom gives a basic answer to the problem of suffering, it still leaves a lot of questions. Like "How is God working with us?" and "What does redemption look like?" For those, we will have to continue our journey.

As you emerge from the wheatfields, you see a river before you. You head for it.

Continue your journey by exploring divine action.
(Turn to p. 64 [ch. 23].)

CHAPTER 10

God at War

You enter the woodlands, through the aspen, rowan, oak, and ash. The walk is pleasant at first, but you begin to hear sounds that concern you. Loud bangs, cries, and the clash of metal invade the peace of the trees. Moving carefully, you approach the commotion and find that at the end of the wood is a battlefield. You cannot tell who is winning, but you know which side you want to be on. Suddenly, you hear hoofbeats approaching from behind, and realize you are directly in the path of a cavalry charge!

The world is a battlefield, and we are caught in the middle. The Bible is full of stories about God at war. In the Hebrew portion of the Bible, God is constantly calling Israel to join the fight against other gods, whether that be Baal, Asherah, or the gods of Egypt. A chaotic water monster, called Leviathan and sometimes Rahab, is God's defeated opponent in stories about creation (Ps 74:14; 89:10; Isa 51:9). These are the spiritual enemies of God's people.[1]

Demons, as such, weren't a big thing in the Hebrew Bible. In the New Testament, however, Jesus is constantly running into them.

1. In the book of Job, the satan (or "accuser") is a member of the heavenly court rather than an enemy of God. His job was as an official prosecutor rather than being a rebel angel on the outside of things.

He's chasing them out of people left, right, and center—silencing them, sending them out, and casting them into swine.

The apostle Paul, for his part, also sees many of the struggles of life as a result of demonic corruption. He writes in Ephesians 6:12, "For our struggle is not against flesh and blood, but against the rulers, against the authorities, against the powers of this dark world and against the spiritual forces of evil in the heavenly realms."

There are advantages to this approach. Clearly God does not intend evil. That is the work of God's enemy instead. It also helps answer the question of why life has always been competitive and violent, even before humans were around. Why was the saber-toothed tiger aggressive or the dinosaur fierce? The timeless fallen angels could have been around mucking things up and disrupting God's harmonious creation all through its development.

There are also difficulties with this view. Why is so little said about demonic influence in Genesis 1? Why is the creation always called good and ascribed to God's work? For example, "The earth is the Lord's, and everything in it, the world, and all who live in it" (Ps 24:1). If disease is due to demons, why do so many ailments respond to medicine? It is difficult to imagine that demons would be afraid of antibiotics or antipsychotics. But perhaps demons are only indirectly responsible. They compromise our bodies in the first place, leaving us open to disease, or they tip us over the edge of mental and physical well-being.

At any rate, suffering was not part of God's plan, and God will resoundingly defeat evil. That does raise another question, though: Why doesn't God just defeat all evil now? You might see the answer in Matthew 13, in which Jesus tells the story of the wheat and the weeds. A farmer plants his field with wheat, but an enemy comes at night and sows weeds among them. By the time they've sprouted, the weeds are so intertwined with the wheat that to pull them out would destroy the wheat as well. So the farmer tells the workers to let them grow together, and they will be sorted out at the end of the season during the harvest.

If God destroyed all evil now, it would end history. Each of us has strands of evil running through us like marbling in meat. If God destroyed all evil, it would mean destroying all of us! Instead, God will let the good and the evil grow together in human hearts and human societies and leave the surgery to separate and destroy evil for later.

Does that mean God is just hanging out in the meantime? By no means! God is always active, though not generally in the "smite evil down" way—at least, not yet. What is God up to? You slip in front of a tree, and the heavily armed riders thunder past you without harm.

With great care, you make your way around the battle and continue on your way. You see a river in the distance and make for it.

Continue the journey with God's work in the world.
(Turn to p. 64 [ch. 23].)

CHAPTER 11

God Can't Stop Evil

You take the path that leads to the valley. The road turns sharply down into a gorge that opens up before you. You can feel the strong pull of gravity and begin to speed up, working with the power that invisibly draws you on. You reflect.

Even though God hates evil, God does not have the kind of power to destroy or force. God is love, and "love is patient, love is kind. . . . It is not easily angered, it keeps no record of wrongs. . . . It always protects, always trusts, always hopes, always perseveres" (1 Cor 13:4–7). There are many actions of love, but none of them are controlling. None of them are violent. The same is true of the Spirit. If God is present, the Spirit bears much fruit, but "the fruit of the Spirit is love, joy, peace, forbearance, kindness, goodness, faithfulness, gentleness and self-control" (Gal 5:22–23). God's ways are always gentle. That precludes the possibility of God simply stepping in and destroying evil.

Many people expect God to ride in on a white horse with sword in hand, ready to slay evildoers and sort out the world's problems by force. They expect the wrong things. Jesus showed that God works differently. He did not dominate the Roman Empire with a sword; he hung on its cross. He died a traitor's death. In doing so, he reordered our understanding of power.

We usually think of people who can force their own will on others as the ones with power. When Jesus died, Caesar seemed like the powerful one. He had armies and governments and money and slaves—all the trappings of power. But no one serves Caesar today. Billions still follow Jesus. Who was, and is, the more powerful?

God's ways are not forceful, but they are powerful. God's power is found not in forcing events to happen. Rather, it is in gently drawing us to a different way of living. God woos creation toward greater harmony. In the meantime, God suffers with us. Every hurt, every tear, every sorrow—God understands everything you have walked through. No one else can share such intimacy. God alone doesn't understand you by mere analogy. Most people understand you by how well you can explain your experiences, or by how close your experience is to their own. Only God has seen your situation from the inside, has known *your* pain.

In fact, some people take things a step further and say that God *learns* from our experiences. The world is in the process of becoming itself, and God takes that journey with us. Precisely because the future is not carefully worked out and controlled, all sorts of possibilities could happen. Even God is not quite sure how the story will end; the future is gloriously, precariously, and creatively open. Instead, the future is worked out in partnership with us. Our decisions make a big difference to the outcome of the world. Nothing is fated or predetermined. God will always pursue the good, but we can throw that good off course. Or we can cooperate with God and bring about wonderful things. It is up to us. As one anonymous poet wrote, "Christ has no body now but yours. No hands, no feet on earth but yours. Yours are the eyes through which he looks with compassion on this world. Yours are the feet with which he walks to do good. Yours are the hands through which he blesses all the world."[1]

Ours are the hands. Ours are the feet. God will work creatively with the instruments that are offered freely but will not force anyone to cooperate.

Our trust is placed in God's creative ability to work good out of evil or in our becoming more like God and joining the peaceful restructuring of the world. As we take up the divine example of nonviolence and love, we reduce the overall evil in the world. Perhaps we will draw others into the same imitation of God. One by one, the kingdom of love will conquer—not by force, but by beauty and goodness. Slowly, God is ever at work, drawing each individual human, animal, tree, mountain, germ, and electron toward love and goodness.

You follow the path to the bottom of the gorge and continue to pursue the work of God.

God will attempt to woo all creation toward the good.
(Turn to p. 48 [ch. 17].)

1. This quotation is often wrongly attributed to Teresa of Avila, but it is clear from her collected works that she did not say it. No one knows to whom the quotation really belongs.

You Meet a Monk

You take a path into the oak woods ahead. As you walk through the ancient oaks, your feet gliding along the silent moss underneath, you see a portly statue of a man with long monastic robes in black and white. Walking closer, you notice a man—this one wearing grey robes—standing and looking up at the statue. Upon greeting him, you inquire about the statue. "This is a friend of mine," he explains, "a friar who wrote *a lot* of theology." (Friar Tuck from *Robin Hood*, by contrast, brewed a lot of beer.)

The man continues, "His name was Thomas Aquinas. He wrote so much and was such a complex thinker that people rarely agree on what he said. But when it came to the question of evil, he said something like the following.

"God causes everything that exists, and humans have perfect freedom. Why then is there evil? There are two reasons. First, there is evil that happens to people, and second, there is evil that is chosen by people.

"Evil that happens to people might have many sources, but most of them are not themselves evil. Rather, they are a conflict of goods. Two musicians could be playing very good songs. But if they play them loudly in the same small room, the conflict will not be good. Or if you had two different sports games, say rugby and football, happening on the same field at the same time, there is going to be conflict. My hungry stomach and the continued life of a lettuce are also set in a type of conflict, but both my being a living person who can get hungry and the life of the lettuce are good things. The type of world God made involves the possibility of these sorts of conflicts. They are unavoidable. Often we suffer because two good things collide in a way that ends up being bad, like putting too many (good) chilis on your (good) pizza. God creates the good things, but their combinations can have bad effects.

"The other kind of evil is evil we experience because people make evil choices. According to Aquinas, evil choices are good actions that are misdirected or wrong for the particular context. This evil is the *lack* of good timing, good judgment, or good intention. God makes us human, but we can choose to be less than fully human, and that is how evil emerges. Let me try to explain. We are in sunlight here. Take your hands and make them into a hollow ball, as if you were trying to hide a golf ball in your hands. Now peek inside. What do you see? Darkness. Did you *create* darkness by folding your hands together? Not really—you just blocked out the light. Darkness isn't something you create in the same way you can generate light. You don't set a darkness fire to spread the dark. You merely block the path of created light. God can create more light, but God can't eliminate the possibility of darkness.

"Just as you folded your hands to create a little patch of darkness, humans can create little pockets of evil by turning in on themselves, like an ingrown toenail. Our actions become contorted and twisted—in short, evil. If we straightened out our lives and acted in the outward and loving way for which we were designed, there would be no problem. But instead of serving God and the world in love, we curl ourselves into knots of self-serving ego. The evil that results is not of God's making.

"But didn't I say Thomas Aquinas believed that God causes our actions *and* that God only causes good? How then could God cause my curling, twisting, contorting actions? This is a bit more difficult. It is like how you can do a good thing, like playing the piano, the wrong way or too much. Playing the piano is fine, but when we play in excess or without proper form, our muscles ache, our tendons tighten, and our arms curl in pain. The twisting in on one's self happens because we are seeking some active good—some pleasure, some skill, some security—in a way that becomes excessive or disproportionate. God directs the good, but the right thing undertaken in the wrong way causes significant harm. God directs and inspires the piano playing, but our own desire to advance too quickly causes the pain. In this sense, God doesn't cause the twisting." The monk, having finished his soliloquy, wishes you well and walks away, singing.

All of this might get God off the hook for *making* evil, you ponder. But it doesn't really answer any questions about how God might be at work to redeem the evil that happens. God may be able to bring good even out of the worst evil. But that is asking a different question.

You have reached the end of this path and this explanation of why there is suffering. You can end here, go back to the last major decision point, or you can go on to ask about redemption.

Go back to the last major decision point.
(Go to p. 1 [ch. 1].)

To explore paths about how God acts in the world, even though these are extra considerations to the basic question of "Why is there suffering?" walk toward a river you see on the horizon. (Go to p. 64 [ch. 23].)

CHAPTER 13

God Exists but Doesn't Love You

You walk along the road and notice how the path arcs slowly to the right. Ahead of you, to your left, is an old oak wood. On the other side, high moorland stretches out on the horizon. Between these is a flat road leading on and up into heathland. You pull out a snack and begin to eat, enjoying the refreshing sense of sugar in your system. Walking and eating always gets you thinking.

The world is a mess of good and evil, pleasure and pain. The world is a random storehouse of nightmare and paradise because God, though powerful, is not particularly interested in fashioning it one way or another. There seems to be no sense in why heroes fall or dictators rule. God exists, but not in order to exert moral force on the universe or to bring the project of creation to a particular end. There are two different reasons why this might be the case.

First, you may believe God is entirely neutral to questions of morality or good. God is not bothered with whether we do good or evil. If we do good, God will meet us in the good. We will find that if we love people, our love often produces loving people. Kindness begets kindness—not because of any work of God but because that is how people are. We will also find that if we do evil, God will meet us in the evil we do. If we are untrustworthy, we lose the ability to trust others, and we create our own suffering. If we threaten or hurt others, we will find that the world is full of threats. God is neutral, or perhaps more accurately, God is a bit of everything. God doesn't cause good or evil; God simply enables everyone else. People reap the consequences of their own actions.

Second, you might think the world is mixed because God is basically uninterested in us. Think of God as the universal architect or the perfect watchmaker. God made space-time, wound the universe up into a singularity, and then let the Big Bang go. God designed the laws of physics, but he is not watching over us. God is unimaginably distant in this view. God isn't paying attention to us at all. We are too small and too insignificant to even capture a bit of divine notice.

There is one last option if you have gotten on this path for a different reason. You might think that God is absolute goodness and love, but that God doesn't *feel* love for us. In that case, you are not going to like this path, and you should probably take the escape route I'm offering back to Thomas Aquinas's views and the oak wood.

Which way would you like to go?

God is neither good nor bad; God is entirely neutral. (Turn to p. 38 [ch. 14].)

God is uninterested in us. (Turn to p. 45 [ch. 16].)

God *is* love, but God doesn't *feel* love. (Turn to p. 33 [ch. 12].)

CHAPTER 14

God Is Neutral

As you walk along the road toward the heathland, you meet a bard. He is a joyful fellow and speaks with an accent from a distant island, and you are thankful for his company. "For two pennies, I'll tell you a tale that will help you on your quest!" he says. Amused by the nominal amount and the formal "bardness" of his manner, you reach into your wallet and draw out a few copper pieces and hand them over. He walks alongside you and begins to tell his tale.

"There was an old and wise woman who sat on the road between two villages. A traveler between the two villages came up to her and asked, 'What are the people like in the village up ahead?'

'How did you find them in the village you just left?' she asked in return. The stranger replied readily, 'Oh, they were wonderful! I found everyone to be generous and kind. People were helpful, gentle, and welcoming.'

'Excellent!' responded the old woman. 'You will find them much the same ahead of you.' Encouraged, the stranger set off down the road.

Two hours later, another traveler came along the road in the same direction as the first. 'What are the people like in the village up ahead?' the stranger inquired.

'What were they like in the village you just left?' the woman asked. The traveler flushed red and responded in a frustrated tone, 'They were angry and cruel. Everyone was aggressive and lazy. They were untrustworthy and unkind. I'm sure I shall never return to such a place.'

'Ah,' sighed the old woman, 'I'm afraid you will find them much the same ahead of you.' The stranger trudged on."

The bard finishes his tale and turns to you.

"Do you understand? God is like the road. (You missed that the road was a main character, didn't you?) God carries us on our journeys and makes our travel possible. But what we find on our journeys is entirely up to us. God is the wellspring of life and the grim reaper. God is the yin and the yang. God won't compel us to do right or punish us if we do wrong. God will simply *be*. Undergirding all action, God is the ground of all being. In God we 'live and move and have our being' [Acts 17:28]. But if you are not looking with careful attention, you might easily miss that there is a God at all."

The bard then bows deeply and walks in the direction from which you came. You continue to turn over the story in your mind.

God will not swoop in to save us from suffering. God will keep creating, and we will keep living, acting, suffering, and dying. Suffering has come about not because God intends it but because it is useful to our biological well-being. Our pain systems evolve, and they warn us of harm that would otherwise be done to us. God doesn't interfere with these evolutionary developments, even if they hurt us. God's view is the cosmic one, embracing the farthest reaches of the galaxies and the silent hurts of our hearts. But God is on the side of neither the apes nor the angels. If our choices or changes lead to suffering and death—well, that is the way of things.

God as the source of life might inspire our devotion. God evokes a sense of transcendence and wonder. But God doesn't require or want worship. In fact, God is unfussed about religion in general. If common worship happens to satisfy your needs, great! If wandering under the stars or walking along the beach alone feeds your soul, perfect. But don't blame God when lightning strikes or disease runs rampant. God is cheering just as much for the virus as for the human.

Is there a solution when it comes to suffering? It is not in God's nature to worry about suffering, but given that it is in *our* nature to want answers, you can look at some of the options for those who don't think God will provide a final answer.

You notice an old pine wood off to your right. Abandoning the journey into the heathland, you head for the forest.

Continue your journey to non-Christian forms of redemption. (Turn to p. 51 [ch. 18].)

CHAPTER 15

God Doesn't Exist

You take the road toward the high moors. As the land rises under you, the air cools into a brisk breeze. It feels like you can see forever without trees or buildings to block your sight. The scenery is bright and beautiful here on top of the world, your surroundings marked by stark colors and contrasts. It is a perfect place to philosophize.

God doesn't exist. There is no divine being of any description. Or perhaps, more gently, there is no positive evidence that would influence us to believe in one god over another. Zeus and Yahweh are both cultural constructions. Religion is a projection of human hopes onto the heavens. The universe is a result of cosmic chance. If we ask why we are here, the only answer is what American scientist Edward Tryon once said: "Our universe is simply one of those things which happen from time to time."[1]

There is still a good deal of mystery wrapped up in this view. Every time we discover more about the world, we find new layers of existence, new and uncharted territories that confound us. Who could have predicted the quantum world? Dare we imagine a universe—or

1. Edward P. Tryon, "Is the Universe a Vacuum Fluctuation?," *Nature* 246 (1973): 296–97.

a multiverse—bursting with alien life? Even our own existence is an unlooked-for wonder, and we have not even begun to scratch the surface of mysteries like the nature of our own consciousness.

However, without a divine presence, without a designer, it is little wonder that the world is stacked with suffering. In fact, scientifically speaking, suffering is an advanced product of life; our ability to feel suffering has been honed over countless generations because it is an advantage to survival. We suffer physically because pain teaches us how to stay alive in a physical world. We learn not to put our hands in fires or walk on broken legs because those things *hurt*. Suffering, however brutal, teaches us our physical limits. We also suffer emotionally because it teaches us how to live in large groups. We learn to cooperate because ostracism and betrayal *hurt*.

Why is cooperation worth the pain of suffering? Because working in groups is a huge advantage to survival. It helps for hunting, agriculture, and protection for a start. Perhaps even more importantly, living in groups allows for knowledge transfer through cultural practices. Our ability to get along with one another means that not everyone has to reinvent the wheel, the airplane, or the iPhone. Most of us have no idea how our computers work or how food gets to our tables. We can benefit from the internet, stable food sources, clean water, and advanced medicine because humans are astoundingly good at working together in large groups.

But those advantages come at a cost. In order to get along, we have to learn how to conform to a wider society's laws and norms. Humans use emotional and sometimes physical pain to set and reinforce the boundaries of what is considered appropriate social behavior.

Many times, these boundaries are set at inappropriate or arbitrary places and can be changed. So far, no one has discovered an ideal set of laws for human cooperation. Philosophers and theologians have argued from time immemorial about whether there is any objective or universal set of morals that would guide the perfect life in community. Complete anarchy—everyone doing what they think is best—loses for us all the advantages of working together. But set any boundary of constraint, and some people will inevitably disregard it. Then the wider group has to decide how to treat the person who has broken the acceptable boundaries, and the questions of law and justice arise.

From an atheist perspective, laws don't reflect universal or eternal moral principles. They are useful tools to help people get along with each other. They can and should change with the times. Atheists tend to look to the sciences to help us determine how to create good laws. For example, studies can show which policies benefit the most people under certain circumstances. Medical sciences can help improve health and provide a vision of physical flourishing. But even those get us only so far.

The scientific method is the best path to truth that humans have yet developed, but it is not perfect. Science is influenced by social constraints, human personality, the honesty of its practitioners, and the reach of our technology. Science doesn't tell us the unvarnished truth about the world, but it does give reliable testimony to much of the best sense we can make of life. Science cannot give us all the answers to questions we might ask. But it can give solid reasons for why we suffer. Earthquakes happen because of plate tectonics. Cancer happens because of genetic mutations. Without plate tectonics and genetic mutations, we wouldn't be here to start with, so there is little reason to complain about the occurrence of these things. Science can also offer powerful solutions. Doctors can find cures, preventions, and powerful pain relief. Engineers, meanwhile, can save even more lives than doctors by building earthquake-proof buildings and creating clean water sources.

Atheism does not have a monopoly on the sciences. Although in much of the Western world, more scientists are atheists than otherwise, science is practiced by people of every faith and creed. What atheism rejects are the "happily ever after" stories that religious beliefs often hold. There is no *deus ex machina*, no god or supreme power who will one day redeem and make whole what we ve left broken.

If the world is going to be healed, we must step up to the plate. What does atheism mean for future hope? You walk toward a pine forest on the horizon.

Continue to non-Christian redemption.
(Turn to p. 51 [ch. 18].)

CHAPTER 16

God Is Not Interested

As you walk, the landscape around you transforms into gently rolling hills covered in heather and gorse. You can hear the larks singing from their hidden nests. Walking among the heath is pleasant at this time of year. You amble and let your mind freewheel, turning like the swifts far overhead.

God exists but is not particularly interested in our lives or our world. God is not personal. The universe shows the evidence of a creator: it is ordered and logically built. Everywhere we look we can see the fingerprints of creation. The universe seems fine-tuned for life, and the laws of nature provide a predictable and rational environment for us to inhabit. But while the fingerprints of God are everywhere, God's hand is nowhere to be seen. It was removed long ago.

Imagine a watchmaker creating a watch. She will spend long stretches of time planning the inner workings. She will carefully grind out the gears and gather the screws and springs that will lend motion to the wheels. The master watchmaker may spend years designing the movement and parts. But once the watch is assembled, the master craftswoman no longer has her fingers on the cogs. The watch is closed and runs on its own. If the watchmaker is skilled in her work, the watch will run without the need for any further intervention.

God does exist and did create the world. We don't know how long God spent planning the Big Bang or the course of evolution. That may have taken eternities. But when God finally set off the singularity that created the universe, God also stopped working within it. God does not interact with the world in any way. If the world is watched by a divine figure, it is watched from afar.

When it comes to suffering, then, there is no grand plan. God will not intervene to save us from or to redeem our suffering. We suffer for natural reasons: because of an accident, the limitations of our physical bodies, or the malicious behavior of others. God neither intends our sufferings nor works to make them meaningful.

The best God does is to give us the capacity of reason so we can make meaning ourselves. We can use mathematics and science to uncover the ordered natural laws. We can use psychology and neurobiology to understand our own minds and behaviors. These teach us about how God ordered the world so we can get along with the world as best as possible. We can use medicine to reduce suffering, physics to increase the safety of transportation, and AI to create robots that take on dangerous jobs. But when we die, we die. There is no afterlife, no future hope of resurrected existence. Those were just stories created by people with fanciful imaginations who wanted to motivate us beyond our own fear. Jesus was a great teacher who could see deeply into the nature of things. But he was no messenger of God, no harbinger of a loving Supreme Power. Like every other human, he died and passed away. Likewise, the Bible is not a special message from God; it is just another book written by people to describe God. It got some things right and many things really, really wrong.

We can become like God by using our rational faculties. They are what distinguish us most sharply from animals. We can use our reason to figure out the laws of nature, to understand the mechanisms of this world. Once we unlock those secrets, we can begin to play with the possibilities of the world. Nuclear power can provide vast amounts of energy from miniscule amounts of matter. People can jet across the world in a matter of hours—journeys that once took months or years to accomplish. Formerly incurable diseases that were death sentences are now eliminated or simply set us back a couple of pills. Miracles happen all the time, but we ourselves are the miracle workers through the steady application of God-given thinking.

God has also given a moral grain to the universe. There is a right and wrong, but God will not police the boundaries. If we cross the moral lines that exist, it will be like ignoring gravity: someone will probably get hurt. Religious traditions safeguard and teach moral truth, and the practice of religion may be a noble and honorable thing. But we should remember that God is never going to pay the slightest bit of attention to us, nor is there any hope beyond death. The best religious practices will realize that what we are after is simply an uncovering of the moral laws of the universe, just as the scientist uncovers the natural laws. Religion, prayer, and all the trappings of religious practice don't change God, but they do change us in profound and life-transforming ways.

You follow the road up through the heath and toward a pine forest ahead.

Continue to non-Christian forms of redemption.
(Turn to p. 51 [ch. 18].)

CHAPTER 17

God Woos Creation

You reach the bottom of the valley. High walls rise up on either side as you continue to follow the widening vale. Suddenly, the walls fall away, and you are once again on open land. A pine forest is away to your right, while the road to your left you cannot quite see, but you see glimpses of distant buildings that gleam in the sunlight. You squint up at the sky, the unveiled sun blinding you, as you think.

The effect God has on the world is like the sun's influence on the earth. The attractive power of gravity silently and continually keeps the earth in orbit. The sun doesn't reach out to the earth and interfere with its motion. The sun simply *is*, and its existence is enough to keep the earth in orbit. The sun and earth have kept the same relationship for billions of years. One burns brightly in the center, while the other spins around it, pulling away yet transfixed by the sun's presence. This relationship won't last forever. Eventually, one force will win over the other. The earth will finally fall into the sun. Or perhaps some great space body will collide with the earth, violently forcing it out of its well-worn course. Energy will surpass gravity, and the earth will spin out toward the icy realms where gas giants rule the heavens.

Just as the sun attracts planets, God draws people to God's

own self—not by messing with their freedom but simply by merit of being God. Like the pull of gravity, people are drawn toward the divine life, toward joy, toward love. Unlike the earth, people have a choice about how they respond. They can turn toward the divine invitation, or they can resist it. Also, unlike the sun, God can try different possibilities to draw us to goodness and love. In reality, God is not like the sun in many crucial ways—an impersonal and inert ball of matter. Rather, God is the true lover of all created things. God is the only one who does not love out of any self-interest. God is every being's soulmate.

One remarkable aspect about lovers is how often they spend their time waiting. Romeo waits in the garden for Juliet to emerge onto her balcony. Dante waits nine years for a second meeting with Beatrice. Princess Fiona waits in the dragon-guarded keep for her prince to rescue her (this, despite the fact that she is more than capable of rescuing herself). Lovers take action, but each action must always be followed by waiting. The lover waits to see if the actions are responded to, taken up by the beloved. Then, precariously and without assurance of success, the lover responds and acts once more to romance the beloved more fully.

Romance offers us our most obvious forms of wooing. God's wooing is slightly different from ours, because the more we are drawn into the divine sphere of influence, the more we become ourselves. The more we turn away from God's invitation, the more distorted we become. This is kind of like how a good mirror shows us for what we are in all our uniqueness, but a curved mirror makes everyone into the same odd shapes. Looking to God reveals us as we are.

The great question, then, is whether we will look and whether we will follow. When the silent invitation tugs our hearts toward the act of love, will we respond? God's intention is to draw every element of creation—from quasars to quarks, and every living creature—into the embrace of divine love. At this point in history, no one knows if God will succeed or not (not even God!).

What do you think? Does God succeed in drawing all creatures into divine love?

God succeeds! Head for the distant gleaming city.
(Turn to p. 122 [ch. 41].)

God does not succeed. Turn for the pine woods.
(Turn to p. 51 [ch. 18].)

CHAPTER 18

Non-Christian Redemption

You approach a thick pine wood. The road is broad and clear, and you enjoy meandering along. There is no hurry, although you cannot see where the road will lead. It is pleasant to walk under the patient trees; you feel a peace here in the living world. Eventually you arrive at a crossroads with four paths leading in different directions under the boughs.

Christians believe in a personal God who is interested in the world and will someday act with power and intention to make all things right. If you have ended up here, you have not followed that path.

So if God is not going to swoop in and save the day, what are the options for meaning and hope?

The first possibility is that meaning is self-made. While there is no cosmic force that will determine the meaning of things, we can make meaning in our own lives. Sure, it is temporary, but so is everything! It is better to get on with enjoying life than to spend too much time worrying about fitting in with invisible and undetectable rules of the universe. Insofar as meaning exists, it is entirely what we make of it.

The second option is that hope is found in how we invest in lives beyond our own. Even if we think our own life is meaningless, when we die our bodies will decay and become food for other creatures. Their lives will depend on and be fed by the end of ours. The molecules of our bodies, once forged in the heart of a long-dead star, will go on to be part of the ocean, the skies, and countless other organisms. Whether we like it or not, we are part of the great circle of life, and that provides a completely naturalistic context for understanding the greater meaning of life.

The third option is that even without a God, there is still "something else" that we can't quite define. Religion is mostly made-up nonsense, but spirituality points us in the direction that there is some greater but undefinable existence that draws us up into greater meaning.

The fourth and final option is simply to protest the possibility of meaning. Even if we can make meaning of life, because of God or whatever, it comes at too high a price. Any universe or deity, any meaning-making attempt that demands the cost of suffering we see around us, deserves rebellion, not cooperation. We should protest any system of thought that tries to say, "It's all worth it in the end." Hand back your ticket to that final harmonious vision; it is compromised by the blood, sweat, and tears of this mortal vale.

It is time to decide. Which path will you follow?

Meaning is self-made. (Turn to p. 56 [ch. 20].)

We are part of the circle of life. (Turn to p. 59 [ch. 21].)

Spirituality directs us into mystery.
(Turn to p. 61 [ch. 22].)

Protest. (Turn to p. 53 [ch. 19].)

CHAPTER 19

Protest

You take the path marked "Protest."[1] It arrives at a cliff of sheer rock, rising from the forest floor. In the side of the rock face you see a cave. It is large and dry and provides a place of retreat and withdrawal from the comforts you left behind you. Settling in, you begin to think.

Why would anyone in their right mind want to find comfort in the idea that God or some other ultimate destiny will make all things well? Pie-in-the-sky thinking might be a comfort to some, but it is a horror story for those who have moral sensitivity and who bother to think about the whole thing carefully.

How so? As soon as you think about it, any god who would put us through hell on earth for some greater good is a moral monster. Want proof? You remember the thought experiment composed by Russian novelist Fyodor Dostoevsky and by American author Ursula Le Guin and bring it to mind once more.

You imagine a town that is a perfect society. Everyone is at peace. Joy fills every day, and a golden sunset crowns each evening

1. This is the only chapter that has a graphic depiction of suffering. The suffering is fictitious, but I will give you the heads-up now in any case.

into a quiet night of unbroken rest. People work, share, and study to the degree they wish, and everyone wishes just right so that everyone has enough, and no one is in need. People are kind. No one feels ostracism; even microaggressions are unknown. Everyone knows everyone else and are themselves fully known. There is no loneliness, no boredom, no hurt, no oppression. Sex is shared, not taken or forced. Possessions are treasured but not hoarded. The restlessness and uneasiness that drive us forward in ambition or fear of scarcity are unknown. Love reigns supreme.

You would walk in wonder through that society, finding that skepticism is unwarranted and that cynicism seems naive. Your guide shows you the unbroken harmony, even behind closed doors, of the population. They really are that happy. You stay and participate for months, and they are the happiest people you have ever known. Goodness is easy here. No jealousy, no fear, no anger ever mars your perfect enjoyment. But then, one day, you ask the man who was your guide, "How is this possible?" The first shadow you have seen falls across the guide's face. In a lowered voice, he says, "Follow me."

Outside the town, there is a lone shack. You enter, noticing the chipped paint on the door and the dirt covering the surfaces. You catch your breath at the sour smell of decay hanging over the place. A set of wooden stairs takes you into the dark and fetid basement. A slow wail catches your ear—a wail of despair.

The guide unlocks a black door, and behind it is a small child. A little girl, maybe three years old, is chained to the wall, sitting in her own feces. Bright light—now streaming through the door—blinds her, and the wail turns to a sharp yelp of pain.

You ask in horror, "What is this? How could this child be subjected to this?" and the guide answers, "She is the key to all our joy. Each year, an innocent child must be chosen to experience all the fear, loneliness, hatred, and envy that the rest of us are spared. She will only be here one year, and then she will join the rest of the community to experience joy for the rest of her life. But if we took her out, all the evils of normal society would return upon us. All shall be made well for her in another six months' time."

What would you do? Could you go back to your harmonious life, knowing the suffering of one small child was the foundation for all the rest?

Or would you walk away from that perfect life, refusing all the joys and harmonies for the love of one small child, innocently tortured? Would you hand back your ticket to such a paradise?

Many solutions to the problem of suffering say something like, "We suffer now, but we will have joy in a future state. Our suffering now is the key to joy then." But the God who would put us through hell now for whatever glorious eternity later is a moral monster on par with those who participate in the imaginary town. Even if there was such a God, the moral person would refuse to take part in that God's heaven. They would hand back their ticket. Any resolution to the problem of suffering that relies on a future peace is meaningless.

You have reached the end of this path, this explanation for suffering. You may end your path here or return to the last major decision point.

I'll finish here. I need to protest for a while.

Return to the pine forest. (Turn to p. 51 [ch. 18].)

CHAPTER 20

Meaning Is Self-Made

The path marked "Self-Made Meaning" leads you to a wide pastureland. Several small woods interrupt the line of the horizon, and streams meander bucolically through the fields. A few cabins are dotted across the landscape. There are others here, but none press so closely that you would be crowded. Everything is just right; all you need to do is get to work to make a home.

When it comes right down to it, life is what we make of it. That can be a hopeful outlook. Nothing is written into the fabric of the cosmos, nothing is determined. No universal power is looking out for us, but neither is any universal power domineering our future. We are required to use all our ingenuity, creativity, passion, and skill to create the best life we can. Suffering is a basic fact of human existence. Our social evolutionary heritage also means that meaningful relationships, love, and community are part of our experience. We are social animals, and much of our meaning in life comes from how we live with one another.

While there is no ultimate purpose to life, we can find proximate meaning in many things. We can enjoy the good things around us: good food, good drink, good friends. We can find meaning in helping one another, in learning and education, and in creating works of beauty.

Our legacy can be found biologically in our children. By passing on our genes, we pass on a unique piece of life's history that is unrepeatable. By the same token, what we do to help and preserve the lives of others—whether human or nonhuman—also contributes to the ultimate shape of life on earth.

Our legacy can be crafted through works of art, literature, film, technology, and song. Humans are creative beings, and the way we see the world can be preserved and passed on in many ways.

Quite apart from all these possibilities, it may be that our legacy will simply be forgotten. Our life is a brief flash. No ancestor will remember us, and no future historian will read our name. But perhaps, as English author Mary Ann Evans (aka George Eliot) said of her most famous character from *Middlemarch*, "The effect of her being on those around her was incalculably diffusive: for the growing good of the world is partly dependent on unhistoric acts; and that things are not so ill with you and me as they might have been, is half owing to the number who lived a faithfully hidden life, and rest in unvisited tombs."[1]

A faithfully hidden life can be a well-lived and satisfying life, and it can add some small measure to the growing good of the world. Those who lived this way and then have died do then, of course, decompose in an unvisited grave. It is, after all, the fate of everyone eventually. The star we revolve around will explode and consume the whole earth. Even if humanity gets to the point where we can move to other solar systems and other galaxies, someday the universe will either stretch out into a heat death or implode in a

1. George Eliot, *Middlemarch* (London: Penguin, 1994), 838.

"Big Crunch." At that point, all life, intelligence, and meaning will be destroyed.

You breathe deeply and set out to build, ready to enjoy your life.

You have come to the end of this path.

To explore other options of non-Christian redemption, turn back to p. 51 [ch. 18].

CHAPTER 21

Circle of Life

You take the path marked with a circle. It leads out of the woods and onto a vast grassland. A great stone structure rises from the otherwise flat plain. A memory stirs in your mind.

You remember the scene from *The Lion King* when Simba and Mufasa are having their morning lesson. Mufasa is preparing his son for the eventuality of his own death, but then goes on to talk about how a king must understand the delicate balance of life and have respect for all the other creatures.

"But Dad, don't we eat the antelope?" Simba interjects.

"Yes, Simba, but let me explain. When we die, our bodies become the grass, and the antelope eat the grass. And so we are all connected in the great Circle of Life."[1]

The path from lion body to grass is a bit more complicated than Mufasa makes out, but the essential idea is right. Although nature is often characterized as wasteful, the truth is that nothing at all is wasted. Every death feeds new life. Every time a balance is broken, a new balance is eventually found.

1. Roger Allers and Rob Minkoff, directors, *The Lion King* (Burbank, CA: Walt Disney Studios, 1994).

Your body is 18.5 percent carbon, every molecule of which was forged in the heart of a star that exploded more than five billion years ago. Your body is made of stardust. The water that hydrates you has been part of oceans, rivers, clouds, and countless other organisms. When you die, your body will become part of countless more.

When we say that those who have died are still with us, we could take this to quite a literal degree. Some of the water molecules in your body were once part of Napoleon's body. Some others were part of Buddha's. And Jesus's. Your body will go on to be part of countless new organisms, human and nonhuman, for the billions of years the sun has left to burn. Once it explodes, our cosmic dust will be scattered across the universe and may well end up becoming part of some new planet.

Knowing this bigger story doesn't make our pain in suffering or the parting of death any less acute. We still suffer. Yet it does mean that none of us is without context or meaning. We are all part of history. Whether we know it or not, our life is essential to the lives of countless others. Both in life and in death we serve the flourishing of other life. Whether we know it or not, others will be thankful that we lived.

You have come to the end of this path.

To explore other options of non-Christian redemption, turn back to p. 51 [ch. 18].

Existence Is a Great Mystery

The path marked "Mystery" leads you out of the woods and into a wildflower meadow. A soft breeze stirs the brightly colored carpet of flowers. The wind seems to blow peace through your own heart also, and, listening, you can almost make out the words couched in the murmur of the wind. You relax into this familiar mood.

When you've climbed a mountain, watched a sunset, or sat in silence for a while, you have discovered something you did not expect. There was a peace—almost a presence. It was not the grandfather-in-the-sky of popular theism. No personality was attached to it. There was simply a conviction that life is part of a bigger whole, a glimpse of a hidden pattern that disappears as soon as it is recognized.

There is more to life than meets the eye. We are busy chasing love, jobs, success, ambitions. All our activity is like the splashing of a rowboat on the ocean. The depths beneath us reveal whole worlds of which we are unaware. Unless . . .

Unless we take the time to stop. Unless we take the time to sense. Unless we clear our minds of all our goals and just observe. Take in the vast scope of reality. Then the magical nature of our reality bears down on us. (Yes, "magical"—no other word will do!)

We make meaning in our own lives, but there is also wider meaning present in the universe that is not of our making. Our self-made meaning is small and poor compared to what we can find beyond ourselves. We are like a child playing with a car we've fashioned from a cardboard box while sitting beside a Porsche. We can join in the wider adventure of the cosmos, and if we are willing, we can tap into those resources.

How do we join that larger story? It is difficult to describe, but it is sort of like being at a professional sports event. Enough fans gathered into one place with one purpose have a sort of transcendent appeal. You are swept up into the atmosphere, drawn along by the enthusiasm of everyone around you. The shared attention of thousands acts like a megaphone of meaning.

The sense of cosmic appeal is kind of like that, except it is not the cheering of football fans that draws you in but the chorus of the stars, the whispering encouragement of the wind, the wild play of ocean waves. The raw, natural power of a mountain, the gentle, quiet beauty of a plowed field, or the almost-audible growing of trees in an ancient forest draws us into the play of life.

If the history of the earth were measured by a twenty-four-hour clock, the origin of life on earth would have happened at about four o'clock in the morning. Algae would have emerged a little after two o'clock in the afternoon. Dinosaurs only emerged at 10:56 p.m. and mammals at 11:39 p.m. Humans would have appeared at 11:58:43 p.m., a little over one minute away from the present. When we get caught up with our nanosecond life spans, we miss the drama of the whole. The life-forms that have ruled the earth for eighteen hours might feel it is a little presumptuous for the seventy-seven-second humans to decide they are the point of it all.

Indeed, with climate change and the threat of nuclear destruction, the human story may not reach seventy-eight seconds. But the bacteria and other single-celled life that fill the earth won't mind our removing ourselves from the biosphere. Some already live on our nuclear waste. Others live well beyond the reach of our power, in the deep ocean or deep in solid rock. We've already accidentally transported life to the moon, left it there for a few years, and brought it back. It was no worse for wear because of the trip.

Douglas Adams suggests in *The Hitchhiker's Guide to the Galaxy* that the earth is secretly run by mice and dolphins. Perhaps it is really run by microorganisms—they are the ultimate reality, and we are simply convenient vehicles for their movement.

I jest, of course. Yet perhaps we need to see the smallness of humanity to get a proper view of ourselves. That is part of the same shift of perception that invites us to turn life into a dance with all other life. We are not alone in the world, and our own self-made meaning is only the echo of a mystical, cosmic play of which we are a part.

Spirit is everywhere. Meaning is everywhere. It just takes a willing participant. You step up to take your place.

You have come to the end of this path.

To explore other options of non-Christian redemption, turn back to p. 51 [ch. 18].

CHAPTER 23

God Creatively Responds

Your road leads to a broad and somewhat muddy river. Trees grow along its banks, casting the bank in shade. Tied to one of the trunks is a small boat. As you approach it, you find a note attached to its bow:

O Pilgrim come and rest awhile,
Come abide in me.
Exchange weary feet for water's glide
And I will help you see
The subtle movement of God's hand
In human hearts and minds
And how God took on human form
And roamed a distant land.

"I suppose I am the pilgrim," you mutter. You step into the boat and then untie it. The water gently bears you downstream, and you pick up an oar to occasionally guide the little craft back to the center of the river. You notice a small pamphlet in the bottom of the boat. You pick it up and begin to read. To sit and read is a welcome relief after the many weary miles of walking.

The Christian God is a God who acts. While others might think of God as distant or uninterested, Christians have always thought of God as one who is intimately at work in the world.

God was first revealed to be at work in creation, spinning out the cosmos—the planets and stars—in all their vast array. But God also acts in each and every moment. Creation was not something that happened a long time ago; it is an ongoing reality. Each instant, God sustains matter and holds together the galaxies and the atoms as faithfully as gravity sticks us to the surface of the planet.

A friend of mine once said she thought God had better things to do than care about us. "He's off taking care of the stars." I disagreed with her. Stars are great, of course, but they are also simple. Big balls of burning hydrogen set in the vacuum of space don't take much caring for—it is not a complex setup. Numberless planets orbit those stars, but most of them are lifeless. Space is vast, but it is not all that interesting.[1] *A careful glance every few hundred millennia will tell you all you need to know. If you want to be involved in the most complex and fast-moving action in the universe, it would be hard to beat our beautiful earth, bursting with life and change.*

God is interested in our lives, our journeys, and our well-being. When we suffer, God is closer to us than anyone else, and God responds to our suffering in creative and redemptive ways.

Sometimes God's actions are hard to see. We expect the heavens to open, the trumpets to sound. We want the king in shining armor to charge in with power and urgency to meet the world's needs. Yet what we find instead are the clouds scudding

1. Astronomy and astrophysics are incredible fields, and so this is not a dig at astronomers. But nothing in space that we know of is as complex as the brain.

across the sky, the sun rising and setting on schedule, and the world rolling on and on.

Where is God?

Some people think God intentionally hides. If the divine power were displayed in full majesty, it would not solve the world's problems. It would strike us dumb, paralyze us entirely, or compel us to obey. Peace would be bought at the price of freedom. The eradication of evil would come at the cost of humanity's destruction. So, God hides. But not entirely. The sun hiding over the horizon leaves an afterglow. Even in the deep of night, the sun's brightness lights the moon and the planets.

God acts—present, yet often unrecognized. In fact, the most important divine act in all of history happened on a sleepy night in a provincial town. A young peasant woman gave birth in a humble dwelling with animals all around. God entered human life. Most people missed it. A few shepherds, a few New Age gurus (traditionally called magi*), and the local livestock were the main witnesses. The world around them slept, while the angels shouted and sang the unfathomable mystery of God come in the flesh.*

He was the carpenter's boy. Born from a shotgun wedding, it was whispered. Stranger stories of heavenly messengers were also passed around. He was just like us. As a carpenter's apprentice, he cried when he missed the nail and hit his thumb with the hammer. He wept at the poverty and sickness that surrounded him. He rejoiced at the unnoticed good deeds that people silently undertook. He fumed at the institutional hypocrites. God walked the earth for three decades, and most people missed it.

I'm rather glad I didn't live in Jesus's day. I think that if I had, I would have missed him too. I tend to like glitz and glamor, going with the crowd. A dusty preacher telling of a kingdom of love and the way of the cross would have passed me by. I would have missed it.

God's most decisive act in history was the incarnation. Very few people saw it coming.

You set the pamphlet back down and reflect.

How do the birth and life of Jesus give us insight into who God is and how God responds to suffering?

You continue to drift down the river.

Continue your journey with the incarnation.

(Turn to p. 73 [ch. 26].)

CHAPTER 24

Into the Rain

You follow the broad path to the right. The road continues ahead: straight, steady, and sure. But the weather ahead looks frightening. Dark clouds loom overhead, turning the bright day black as night. Lightning dances across the sky above, occasionally leaping to the ground in a strong explosion of light. Thunder rolls almost continually, assaulting your eardrums. As you get nearer, the rain begins to pelt down so thick and fast you could almost believe you were under a waterfall. You continue to put one foot in front of the next, pushing against the now roaring wind. You cannot see where you are going, but each footfall takes you one step farther down the road that leads you on.

We are tempted to blame God for the suffering that surrounds us. But what if it is necessary for our own good? We like to think of the earth as our home, a resting place where we can settle in and be comfortable. Insofar as it fails to be comfortable and safe, we want answers. But perhaps that is the wrong way to think about the nature of the world. If heaven is to be our eternal home, perhaps earth is just a training place—a boot camp—getting us into shape for heaven.

Imagine a boot camp where the commanding officer invites you to be at ease. "Sit down and stretch out before a roaring fire.

Let me make you some tea." That doesn't make much sense. The whole point of being at boot camp would be wasted.

Suffering is hard. It strips away our dignity and can leave us gasping for hope, meaning, and purpose. But hidden inside it are the seeds of growth.

Exercise is hard. It too strips away our dignity. It can leave us covered in sour-smelling sweat, gasping for air, and aching for days. But exercise is the path to growth and strength. The breaking down of our muscle fibers is precisely what gives us the opportunity to be rebuilt in a stronger, healthier way.

Our souls are exercised by suffering like our bodies are exercised by weights and treadmills. The training is not pleasant, but it is necessary.

Just as there is no shortcut to physical fitness, there is no shortcut to the type of spiritual fitness God desires us to have. Even God cannot make us perfectly mature in a moment. We are creatures of slow growth and process, and as soon as God made us human beings, the prospect of making us perfect from the start was impossible even for God. Does that sound dubious? Does this limit the perfect power of God?

In fact, the same was true even of Jesus. It is significant that Jesus did not come as a grown man, wholly formed. God came to earth as a baby and had to learn physical skills and moral wisdom. At the end of the only account of Jesus's boyhood, in Luke 2:52 we are told that "Jesus *grew* in wisdom and stature, and in favor with God and man" (emphasis mine). More to the point, we are told in Hebrews 5:8 that "Son though he was, [Jesus] learned obedience from what he suffered." Unlike our learning, which is usually a long and painful process of trial and repeated error, Jesus learned obedience the first time around. *But he still had to learn it!* And part of what taught him complete submission to the Father, according to the Bible, is what he suffered.

Part of what is tricky here is that suffering doesn't automatically result in growth. It provides the opportunity for growth, but just as seeds don't always germinate, so suffering does not always produce good fruit. We can respond in one of two ways to the reality of suffering. We can lament, cry out, protest, and blame God for putting us through such undeserved suffering—and those are often good things to do. And/or we can try to work with the process, to embrace the suffering and play an active part in turning our suffering into something good. The suffering we endure may not be of our own making. We may plainly be victims of circumstance or the evil decisions of others. Yet we can still look for good, for ways to respond to the suffering with redemptive choices that encourage the growth of our spirits.

Through refusing to repay evil with evil, through forgiving those who hurt us, through loving our enemies, through caring for the needs of the world, we are forged into the inhabitants of heaven. Just as silver must be put in hot fires and completely melted down—in one sense, destroyed—in order to be rid of its dross, so God allows us, possibly even wills for us, to enter into fiery trials.

Given the severity of suffering in this world, though, all this only makes sense if there is some sort of redemption after this life. From our perspective, lots of suffering simply destroys people. We see the melting down but not the remaking.

How does the story continue when we look to heaven? You emerge from the storm, soaked and exhausted but with a vivid sense of hope. You look ahead and see a bright aquamarine river stretching across your path. You walk toward it.

Continue to the river. (Turn to p. 102 [ch. 34].)

CHAPTER 25

Into the Fog

Your road bends into a dense bank of fog. The horizon, then the landscape, and finally even the sun disappears. You are surrounded by heavy, wet, grey clouds. But the road stretches on before you, broad and flat. You cannot see where you are going, but you trust the road. As you walk, you muse over the nature of seeing.

The happenings of this world are like a great tapestry that God is weaving. Our stories, our lives, and those of others are like threads. They interweave with each other, get knotted up, begin, and end throughout time. If you look at a tapestry being woven, you will find two very different perspectives available. From the back, all you see is a jumble of knots and loose ends. Everything is a mess—a chaos of color and threads without meaning. But once you flip it over and look at the front, you can see the design that was present all along. The chaos is resolved, and the beauty emerges.

From our place on earth, the "back of the tapestry" is all we see. There is no good explanation for the suffering and evil in the world so far as we can see (and we can't see very far!). From God's place in heaven, on the other side, each thread is being woven into a pattern and plan of divine glory. That is true of the long-lived threads, but it is also true of those threads that seem to have been cut unfortunately short.

The divine plan extends to the brightest threads of moral purity just as it does to the darkest threads of evil and pain. Each one will contribute to the final richness, intricacy, and beauty of the divine project.

There is no useless suffering, no wasted time. No life is wasted, either. Every twist of fate has contributed to a secret design. The lines of our lives are brought together and pulled apart not by random chance or human choice, but by the guiding of a divine hand. Nothing happens that God does not allow.

Someday we will share God's perspective. We will look at the tapestry of history from the front and see the design that was being woven all along the way. We will see why the sorrowful threads were necessary. Until then, our work is simply to trust—to trust that the painful stretching of our lives is necessary for God's plan and that when we see the ways our lives integrate with the bigger picture, we ourselves will rejoice and praise the Great Artist whose masterpieces are our lives.

There are, after all, only two real choices: either God is in control of our lives, or we are in control of our lives. If we are in control, the whole plan could be shipwrecked on the rocks of human pride and foolishness. But if everything is in God's hands, then we can trust not only that all our pain will one day make sense but that God will perform the redemption promised in Scripture. The One who has everything under control will also be able to bring things to perfect completion.

After many hours of disorienting trudging, the fog slowly begins to lift. Ahead, the road leads to a sparkling river, aquamarine in the now bright sunlight.

You walk toward the river.

Continue your journey to the river.

(Turn to p. 102 [ch. 34].)

CHAPTER 26

When God Became Human

You drift down the river in your boat, contemplating the mystery of God. How do we know what God is like? Christians answer by pointing to Jesus. However, when people look at Jesus, their questions about suffering tend only to increase. After all, Jesus does a lot of what we expect God to do. He heals the sick, casts out demons, and raises the dead. However, he didn't come riding in on a white horse at the head of an army, as some people expected him to. He chose instead to hang on a cross as a traitor. That doesn't seem very God-like.

This is where we get into trouble looking at Jesus. He seems full of contradictions, or at least paradoxes. He comes to proclaim good news but then tells people not to share about how he healed them. He is the Prince of Peace, but in John's Gospel he drives malefactors out of the temple with a whip. He doesn't defend himself when scourged and crucified, but he doesn't mince his words when faced with religious hypocrites either.

Jesus's miracles confront some of the world's pain, as we might expect from God's approach to suffering, but the promises he makes seem at odds with any sort of triumphalism. Yes, "Follow me and you will find life" sounds good, but then it is modified by "take up your cross and follow me" and "anyone who wishes to find their life must lose it" (see Mark 8:34–35).

When Jesus heals, it may not be as clear a thing as simply removing people's pain. Think of the people with leprosy whom Jesus heals. If they had true leprosy (now known as Hansen's disease),[1] then Jesus didn't take away their pain when he healed them—quite the opposite. As doctor Paul Brand found out, rumors of leprosy as "rotten flesh" were all wrong. Instead, Brand discovered that leprosy is bacteria taking up residence in pain nerves. When people's bodies try to kick out the bacteria, it causes swelling, which cuts off the blood supply and kills their pain nerves. That is all. When people lose fingers or toes to Hansen's disease, it is not because of some flesh-eating property of the bacteria; it is simply because they cannot feel pain! They do not pull their hands out of fires or off hot stoves. If they break a bone in their foot, they just keep walking on it. Their bodies are like houses that have no fire alarms. Without a warning signal, they assume everything is okay. Slowly, the lack of pain destroys their bodies.

Back to Jesus now. When he healed leprosy, he was likely restoring these people's ability to feel pain. His healing was the opposite of what we expect healing to be. When he raised the dead, they did not live forever—every person brought back to life by Jesus during his earthly ministry walked through the gates of death again.

This raises a question concerning our expectations of God. Should God be in the business of healing every toothache or just the big diseases like cancer? Should God prevent stubbed toes or just hateful speech? If God does all these things, where should God stop? If God heals my bad knee, would that make any sense if God

---

1. New Testament authors may have used *leprosy* to refer to a number of different skin conditions. However, at least some of these people likely had Hansen's disease.

didn't also heal my bad thoughts? If God healed my cancer but left me with my greed, would the world be any better?

As soon as you start looking more closely, it is hard to say, "God should really fix *this*." In reality, *everything* needs to be remade—taken apart and rebuilt from the ground up. God can cover problems with a bit of duct tape here, add an extra screw there, and make a piecemeal job of repair with a few miracles. But what God is really about is the new creation, when this whole world and all its woes will be taken apart, taken up, and remade top to bottom. Miracles, at best, are a stopgap measure of unusual divine action. In fact, they can be a distraction from the everyday work God is always doing.

If you are finished thinking about divine action, you can get out of the boat on the far side of the river and continue on your way. If you want to think a bit more about miracles—to dwell on this topic a bit longer—you can stop on the edge of the river for a picnic, and if you want to think about other forms of divine action, you can proceed down the river.

Where would you like to go next?

I'm done with God's actions in this world; let's talk about redemption. (Turn to p. 102 [ch. 34].)

I want to hear more about miracles. (Turn to p. 79 [ch. 28].)

Miracles are great, but what about when God does not show up in obvious ways? (Turn to p. 76 [ch. 27].)

God Acts in Various Ways

You continue to travel down the river, thoughts turning over in your mind. Suddenly, the water starts rushing quickly, and you find yourself tossed about in the boat as it runs over rapids. Using your oar, you dig deep into the water and navigate through the rocks. You breathe a deep sigh of relief as the river slows once more. The river continues to widen until you find yourself entering a lake. Four small islands dot the surface of the lake, and on the far side you see a dock where you could land the boat. You pause to think of your next move.

Jesus's miraculous but unexpected work during his earthly ministry gave us a picture of God's response to suffering, but what happens when God does not show up in obvious ways? What happens when miracles are not forthcoming, and Jesus is no longer here in the flesh?

We usually think about God's action in two ways. First, we think about when God changes the outcome of a situation: the incarnation, the miracles, and the signs and wonders. Theologians call those events "special divine action." The other way we think of God acting is in the totally reliable, rock-solid activity that happens everywhere and all the time, like God making sure gravity still works or keeping the cosmos in existence. That is called "general divine action."

But some of God's work in the world exists somewhere between these two. These acts of God are not wonders; they don't shine like beacons in the night, proclaiming the work of God in the world. They don't generally intervene to shove history down a path it was not prepared to take. Yet these acts of God are not absent of influence either. They are more along the lines of God accompanying creation. Let's look at each of four options.

First, you can imagine God's presence as an active lure toward the good. God is not running about intervening in stuff; rather, God's effect on our lives is like the sun's effect on the world. It is attractive, life-giving, and ever-present. In England (which parts of this landscape uncannily imitate), the sun is usually cloud-covered. All you need to get people rushing outside is a few minutes of sunshine. There is no messing with their freedom—they go outside of their own volition, but the sun persuades them to head outdoors. In a similar way, God draws us toward the good simply because good is ultimately pleasurable. It is what we are made for, and it feels as good as the sun on our faces.

Second, God can be active in creating the meaning of events. When events happen, they don't come with an interpretation. What seems like a disaster at one point in time may, at another time, seem like a blessing in disguise. A great stroke of luck can end in disaster. How many relationships have been torn apart by the apparent good luck of winning the lottery? How we interpret an event is actually *work*. It is neither automatic nor self-evident. We have to create the meaning of things. That's part of what God is doing in the world: creating meaning out of ambiguous events that don't carry their own interpretation.

Third, it is possible that when tragedy strikes, God suffers with us. This may seem a bit of rubbish—what use is it for God to suffer with us rather than to prevent the suffering? Anyone who has been through something difficult and terrifying alone knows the difference it makes to have someone with you. God is with us, sharing our suffering.

The last possibility is that God is involved in forging our souls through the fires of adversity. When bad things happen, God is creating possibilities that would allow us to grow through our suffering. Nothing is wasted in God's economy. Rather, like a silversmith who allows metals to go through extreme heat to pull out their impurities, God sees the suffering we go through as an opportunity to purify us from all that makes us less than fully human.

You see the four islands in the lake. You are confident that you can visit as many of them as you like before needing to move on. Where would you like to start?

Let me hear more about God's attractiveness. (Turn to p. 83 [ch. 29].)

God makes meaning out of our lives. (Turn to p. 87 [ch. 30].)

God suffers with us. (Turn to p. 92 [ch. 31].)

God forges our souls through suffering. (Turn to p. 95 [ch. 32].)

CHAPTER 28

Miracles

You pull the boat over to the bank, jump out, and pull up the boat after you. It's time for a rest. You pull the pack off your back and bring out the food you've been carrying. Fresh bread, butter, and cheese all come out in quick succession. They are joined by pork pies, sausages, and a variety of veggies with dip (all these are available in gluten-free and vegan alternatives for those who prefer such things). Sparkling water, juice, and wine come out with the food, available as you please. Scones with cream and jam follow the savory. After eating your fill, you lie back, well sated, and muse over miracles.

Miracles have lost their way over the last three hundred years. People used to know that miracles were primarily an act of divine *communication*. They simply meant that God was present and wanted to speak to you. They often, though not always, answered a particular need.

David Hume, the Scottish skeptic, changed all that. For him, a miracle was a breaking of the laws of nature. Laws of nature cannot be broken, he said, so miracles must not happen. Ever since, people have been trying to show how God can act without breaking the laws of nature. Others have abandoned the concept of miracles altogether and opted instead for a God whose only acts are what nature was going to do anyway.

Scientists tend not to be overly fond of miracles. They seem to threaten the power of science to explain the world. And they are difficult, if not impossible, to catch and study. If God is in the habit of doing miracles, how can we trust our experiments? God could have stepped into the lab and messed things up. The hard truth is that scientists cannot be watching every event in rigorous ways. God might be breaking the laws of nature in the space between the words on this page and your eyes *right now*, and no one would ever know. So perhaps the worries of scientists are a bit misguided. God would have no reason to break the laws of nature in order to mess up their experiments. That would have no communicative value, except to communicate the capriciousness of God. But if God is trustworthy, we can trust that God would not mess with science just for the fun of it.

There are also miracles that don't need any laws of nature to be broken at all. *Miracle* comes from the Latin word *miraculum*, which means "a wonder." Wonders interrupt our daily routines, and they force us to pay attention to what is around us. They are unusual, by definition, but not necessarily impossible. Think of some of the biblical wonders, like when Jesus wants to pay the temple tax. He has Peter go catch a fish, and the fish has a coin stuck in its mouth that will pay the bill for both of them. There is no breaking of the laws of physics in this, just an unlikely set of coincidences.

In the Bible, miracles are often referred to as "signs." Think of how a sign works: it holds information that draws our attention to something else. A road sign, for example, lets me know which way I am headed and how far it will be until I get to the next city. It is important to remember that the road sign *is not the city*. In a similar way, a miracle is not God's presence; it simply points us in the right direction toward God.

Sometimes people can get carried away with seeking miracles. If a miracle doesn't happen, people assume God is not present. Equally, people can camp around a miracle, confusing it with the reality to which it is meant to point.

Think of Oxford—the city of dreaming spires. The road signs on the highway outside have a picture of the spires to let you know you are headed to Oxford. But imagine people stopping on the road, taking pictures of the little road signs, and then saying they had seen Oxford. That would be silly! Once you are in the city and the actual towers loom over you, signs are no longer needed. Intimacy with God is often marked by a *lack* of miracles, not an abundance of them. This causes no end of frustration to everyone.

Teresa of Avila is said to have once gotten stuck on a muddy rural road. Some stories say that the carriage she was riding in broke down, leaving her and her companions stranded in the mud and rain. Another tells of her nearly being washed away by floodwaters while leading others on foot down a flooded road. In any case, when she realized she was stuck, she raised up her arms and shook her fists at heaven, saying, "Lord, if this is how you treat your friends, it is no wonder that you have so few."

Miracles, at best, are highly unusual events that may provide a turning point for someone. They point people toward the reality of God, but they are so unusual that there is no danger of them threatening the reliability of science. In fact, given people's propensity to camp around them and be more interested in the miracles than the reality to which they point, it is little wonder that God keeps them rare. When Jesus was handed over to Herod, Herod was initially delighted. He had heard of Jesus and wanted to see what signs he could perform (Luke 23:8). Yet Jesus was silent, giving only himself. When the reality is there, no sign is needed. Herod quickly lost interest and sent Jesus back to Pontius Pilate to die.

You get up and pack away the leftovers from lunch. It is time to get back to the main conversation about suffering.

You launch the boat and climb inside. The river is moving faster now, and your ears catch the sound of rough waters ahead.

What do we do when God does not show up with miracles? (Turn to p. 76 [ch. 27].)

CHAPTER 29

Divine Lure

You approach the northernmost island. It is a serene little place. Trees provide shade, and wildflowers grow through the grass, creating a multicolored carpet for you to walk on. The air is scented with lavender. In the center of the island is a sculpture. You cannot quite make out what it is at first, but as you look closer you realize it is hundreds of little carvings, each one showing a story of human love. They all connect together into a large Penrose triangle. You can't quite take your eyes off it, and you walk around it, trying to figure out the perspective of it. From every side, it is perfect and impossible.

God is attractive. Goodness is attractive. Beauty is attractive. Something deep in the human soul seeks after these things as naturally as sunflowers follow the arc of the sun. Episcopal priest Robert Farrar Capon takes the analogy one step further: "What [God] does to the world, he does subtly; his effect on creation is like what a stunning woman does to a man."[1] We usually assume that God's work in the world involves seeing some events unfolding and

1. Robert Farrar Capon, *The Third Peacock: The Goodness of God and the Badness of the World* (New York: Doubleday, 1971), 57.

then—like a cop or a teacher observing a fight on the playground—stepping in to interfere with the outcome. We think of God as one who uses force to change the outcome of history.

Great beauty does not need to use force; it simply is, and things change around its attractive nature. Walk by the *Mona Lisa* in the Louvre Museum, and you will see a large crowd of people, stopped and staring. Beauty has caught their attention, changed the course of their path. Beauty draws in attention and emotion, the whole person. Brutes can compel some types of obedience, but they cannot capture the heart. God is no brute.

What if God's work in the world were not that of the supreme commander but of the ultimate lover? That seems a bit weak, doesn't it? God is simply going to love, be beautiful, and attract the world to goodness? "How well has that plan worked?" asks the skeptic.

It is undoubtedly an inefficient way to work. Yet it can make enduring changes that force will never achieve. Think of the people who, inspired by God's love, made a lasting change in evil's reign.

Saint Francis of Assisi, the lover of poverty and simplicity, meandered along the highways and byways of medieval Italy, preaching to all creatures, from lords to peasants to birds. He gave up a rich inheritance, giving up everything to follow Jesus. When he was confronted that the clothes he was wearing belonged to his father, he took them off, too, and walked out of town naked. He left to rebuild a ruined physical church, brick by brick. Then he rebuilt a ruined spiritual church, heart by heart. He rejoiced in hunger as an opportunity to fast. He shared with everyone he came across. He was marked by unrelenting joy. He has inspired millions to become more human—not by force, but by the attractive humility of love.

Perpetua and Felicitas, two Roman women, one a lady and one a slave, were sentenced to death for being Christians. Perpetua had just given birth, and her child was taken away from her. She was offered both her child and her freedom if she would only denounce her commitment to the way of Jesus, the way of love. But neither she nor Felicitas turned from their intention to follow. They were put in the arena and died sad deaths at the jaws of wild animals and the swords of gladiators. But their peaceful love for one another and even for the gladiators who slaughtered them changed the heart of the watching crowd. They conquered the gladiators and the elite of the Roman Empire, not by force, but by the attractive vulnerability of love.

Nelson Mandela, the first black president of South Africa after apartheid, chose the way of reconciliation rather than revenge. He led an angry and betrayed nation into a new future without the bloodshed of civil war that everyone thought was inevitable. He was heroic in his patience and his love, even for those who had imprisoned him and oppressed the black inhabitants of South Africa. Mandela inspired millions of others to follow his example of refusing to take up arms or to institute harsh retaliatory policies. He changed a nation not by the power of force but by the attractive forgiveness of love.

There are quicker, less costly ways of bringing change: a military coup, a violent crusade, or a new dictatorship. These get the surface of things to change, but they do not change the roots of human motivation. Only love can do that. God, who cannot be tricked by surface-level change, looks for the hearts of people to change. That leaves change by love as the only option.

God stands as the Lover of the world, the one who draws all creatures into love. Perhaps that is why ecosystems work the way they do: every creature relies on other creatures; every life is tuned in to the lives of those around them. Perhaps the ever-growing interdependence of life is a hint of the attractive power of God's love as an animating force of the universe.

Inspired by love, you turn back to your boat. Will you head to another island or move on from divine action?

God makes meaning out of our lives.
(Turn to p. 87 [ch. 30].)

God suffers with us. (Turn to p. 92 [ch. 31].)

God forges our souls through suffering.
(Turn to p. 95 [ch. 32].)

I'm ready to move on from divine action.
(Turn to p. 98 [ch. 33].)

CHAPTER 30

Meaning Making

You approach the northern inner island. It is dominated by a cave set into a rocky hill. At the mouth of the cave is a table with candle and matches. You light the candle and walk in. At first you see nothing, then you see the gleam of another candle in the distance. As you approach it, you discover it is your own reflection in the largest sheet of silver metal you have ever seen, covering the whole back end of the cave. Walking next to it, you see thousands of small scratches that zigzag randomly across the surface. As you bring your candle close, the light catches in the cracks, forming little concentric circles around your flame. Wherever you move, the pattern emerges, then disappears as you move on. Light, you realize, brings order out of the chaos of scratches.

We are used to thinking that the meaning of an event is set in stone the moment it happens. The past is finished, concrete, and unchanging. But perhaps that's not right. The *events* of the past are indeed unchangeable. We can't make something that happened unhappen. The importance of past events, however, can change. There is no easier way to show this than through a famous story called "The Taoist Farmer."

> There once was an old man and his son who owned a horse, which provided their only source of income. One night the horse ran away. The next day, all the villagers trotted out to the old farmer's house and said, "Oh no! This is the worst thing that could have happened to you."
>
> The old farmer quietly answered, "It's too early to tell."
>
> The next day the horse returned with five other horses. All the villagers immediately ran out to the farmer and said, "Congratulations! This is the best thing that could ever happen to you."
>
> But the old farmer quietly said, "It's too soon to tell."
>
> The next week, his son tried to ride one of the new horses. The horse was wild, and it threw him into the corral fence. He broke his leg, could not walk for months, and was left with a permanent limp. The villagers came again and said, "What a terrible tragedy! Those horses were a curse after all."
>
> But the farmer said quietly, "It's too soon to tell."
>
> A year later, the army came through the village to take all the healthy young men off to war. The old farmer's son was of no use to them and was left behind. None of the other young men ever returned.

As each event unfolds, the meanings of the previous events shift back and forth. The horse running away was bad—until it brought new horses home with it. Now the tragic event was simply a precursor to a great good! Without the tragedy, the greater good could not have happened. Yet the triumph is soon stained with new sorrow that could not have happened without the victory. Each new event reshapes the meaning of what has gone before.

The highly fluid nature of the past is why historians generally don't study anything that has happened within the last forty years;

current events are still busy throwing the meaning of the past back and forth. They hope that after a few decades, the meaning of past events will settle down into something that can be trusted to pen and paper.

Even so, the meaning of the past is still highly fluid centuries after it has happened. The history of the world will continue to change right up until the end of time. The same is true of our lives. You may experience instances where a tragic event takes on a new meaning, becoming part of the arc of a good story. You may experience a great good that afterward seems like a mockery in light of a following tragedy. The meaning is fluid.

There is a game I sometimes play with my friend's child: we invent stories together but do it by writing in turns. I might introduce the setting and the main characters in a few sentences and then hand over the notepad to my co-creator. He then adds a few more lines and hands it back for the next plot twist or dilemma to be resolved or complicated by yet another plot twist.

It is hard work! Each time I get a story arc going, it takes a drastic turn for the unexpected. Children are far more inventive than adults, and I would often find myself helplessly puzzled by where we ended up. Sometimes I could bend the story back to the track it was on at first. Sheer inventiveness might return the story to my original intent. However, when a Pokémon makes a sudden entrance into my medieval tale (true story), or when my main character is splatted by a falling boulder, then there is no going back. A whole new meaning must be made.

Imagine God at work in the world as a skilled storyteller who can tell the story of creation with us as co-writers. God not only recounts the events of history but also gives them their meaning. God can write the ongoing story through our lives, asking us to participate in the Great Tale of the world. But, of course, we can also add our own pieces of the story quite apart from God's intentions. We can add alien intrusions—in a sense, that is exactly what sin is—and then God is left to draw back together the threads of the narrative.

God is so talented and creative that God can work many things to the good simply by directing the ongoing story in such a way that the tragedy becomes part of a very good event. It is not that God meant the tragedy to happen all along just so the good event could happen; rather, God's ability to improvise and innovate on our failures means nothing is wasted, nothing is irredeemable. Senseless evil will not be senseless in the end.

With little things, a little redemption will do. A little unexpected turn to the good is more than enough. With great sorrows, however, nothing within the history of a person's life will be able to give it a new redemptive meaning. God's re-creation of meaning will have to wait until the end of history, when the entire creation will be taken apart, cleaned up, and put back together. Then, and only then, will some tragedies be re-created into something sensible. Only then will the meaning be given sufficiently new form for us to do anything other than lament.

When Jesus died, there was nothing good about his death. However, in light of the resurrection, the day of Jesus's death is now remembered as "Good Friday." The scars from the torture he received became marks of triumph carried into the new life. The meaning of them changed from evidence of hatred and tyrannical oppression to the marks of unlimited love. Someday that same transformation will happen to the whole world.

In the meantime, we don't have to try to make meaning out of everything we encounter. That will ultimately be God's job. We are free to accept tragedy as tragedy without looking for a silver lining. We may see small, shifting patterns now, candlelight catching on random scratches. But when God remakes the meaning, it will be plainly evident. But now we are straying into the realms of redemption, and we haven't left divine action yet!

You leave the cave and get back into your boat. Where to next?

Let me hear more about God's attractiveness.
(Turn to p. 83 [ch. 29].)

God suffers with us. (Turn to p. 92 [ch. 31].)

God forges our souls through suffering.
(Turn to p. 95 [ch. 32].)

I'm ready to move on from divine action.
(Turn to p. 98 [ch. 33].)

CHAPTER 31

God Suffers with Us

You row your way over to the central, southern island. A slight mist covers the trees and the dark-colored rocks, curling about in small vortices. When you walk into it, you are struck by an intense, sweet odor. It strikes you in an instant that this is not a natural mist but is incense, sweeping through the trees. You set out to look for the source.

When we suffer, God is right beside us, closer than a doctor, friend, or lover. God alone is always attentive, always present. More than that, only God can fully understand our suffering. Other people can feel suffering for us, but only God can feel *our* suffering.

This brings the comfort of knowing we will never be alone, but it still leaves a lot of questions. If someone breaks their arm and goes to the doctor's office, what help is it if the doctor looks sympathetic and then breaks his own arm so that he is suffering with them? What is needed when we are broken is someone who restores us, not someone suffering in just the same way. So what good is a God who suffers?

It is true that co-suffering doesn't relieve or resolve suffering. But it does vastly reshape the way we imagine God. How? Take an example. Do you remember Lord Farquaad from the movie *Shrek*?

The short little dictator with the huge ego? He wants to rescue Princess Fiona from a distant dragon-guarded keep. But he won't risk the quest himself. Instead, he gathers a group of knights and—while he stands on a balcony far above them—tells them he will send them one by one into peril. "Some of you may die," he says grandly, "but that is a risk that *I* am willing to take."[1] The crowd bursts into applause.

It is complete foolishness, of course. Someone who is willing to risk other people's lives while staying at home safe and sound is not to be admired but reviled. We want the leader who will take the risk with us; we want the God who understands.

God's co-suffering does not relieve our suffering, but it does relieve us of the temptation to imagine that the Creator is like Lord Farquaad. It would be easy to imagine: God created the world with the grand plan of creating humans. If countless creatures die along the way to realizing that vision, well, that is a risk God is willing to take! God remains high above all the ugly chaos, untouched and unmoved by the suffering below. God wants humans to be refined through suffering? Excellent! Another risk God is willing to take. Let them suffer and be made well. God is high above such suffering, ensconced in the glories of heaven.

The idea that God suffers with creatures dispels that vision of the divine. There is no risk, no suffering, that God's creatures undergo that God does not share. Instead, every pain, every loneliness, every death is taken into the heart of God. God knows our pain.

God demonstrated the willingness to suffer alongside us in the cross of Christ. Jesus could have been spared the ordeal of the cross.

1. Andrew Adamson and Vicky Jenson, directors, *Shrek* (Universal City, CA: DreamWorks Pictures, 2001).

When Jesus was being arrested, one of his followers tried to protect him with a sword. But Jesus's rebuke came swiftly: "Do you think I cannot call on my Father, and he will at once put at my disposal more than twelve legions of angels?" (Matt 26:53). Instead of fighting back, Jesus willingly gave himself to the passion—to suffering with and for the world. It is in Jesus's cross that we see God most clearly. God's response to evil was not to miraculously intervene to stop harm. Jesus didn't prevent evil. Instead, he hung beside all the other victims of violence, suffering, pain, and tragedy.

Yet Christ also prefigured the future of all life in his resurrection; death's victory is not final. It is only a temporary delay until all of history is wrapped up.

You follow the thickening mist to the center of the island to a deep volcanic fissure that is billowing out smoke. You see how a tree fell into the vent, and its resin is now creating the incense infusing the island. It rises like a prayer into the sky.

Where would you like to go next? You can keep exploring the islands of divine action, or you can move on.

Let me hear more about God's attractiveness.
(Turn to p. 83 [ch. 29].)

God makes meaning out of our lives.
(Turn to p. 87 [ch. 30].)

God forges our souls through suffering.
(Turn to p. 95 [ch. 32].)

I'm ready to move on from divine action.
(Turn to p. 98 [ch. 33].)

CHAPTER 32

The Garden

You arrive at the southernmost island. A high stone wall circles the small island. In the middle of the wall is a heavy wooden door. You enter, pushing the stiff door open, to find a carefully tended garden inside. Medicinal plants and herbs are carefully set out along the near wall, while vegetables and fruit trees fill the far plots.

You walk along through the herbs and flowers, noticing the variety. Hellebore and sweet honeysuckle grow alongside bitter rue. Each plant is carefully pruned, with new growth emerging from the deep cuts on their stems. You think about the process of pruning.

We are changed by what we suffer. That seems obvious enough. What is perhaps less obvious is that we can choose *how we change* much of the time. If someone treats us unfairly, we can choose to be just as nasty to them or to treat them fairly and kindly nonetheless. One of those choices will be far easier to make than the other, but both are often possible—if only by the grace of God.

One of God's jobs is to use circumstances to help shape us into people who look like Jesus. Suffering is not caused by God, but it can be used by God. Damage caused by accident or malice can be turned into fruitful pruning of our souls. After all, if bad things are going to happen, wouldn't we prefer that God use them?

Wouldn't we prefer that our pain have some sort of chance to make us better and stronger people? It would be better for there to be the possibility of pain being used for good, rather than simply saying it is totally senseless. Maybe its causes were senseless, but once suffering has made its terrible mark, it is better to work with what is left than to abandon experiences or people to the scrap heap of life.

The process of turning people into great souls is not a straightforward one. Despite all the imagery in Scripture of God as a refiner of metals or a potter of clay, personal transformation is not a technology like metallurgy or pottery. A certain kind of metal will always respond to heat in the same way. But people respond very differently to the same circumstances. There is no one-size-fits-all path to personal growth, and some growth happens only through the fires of suffering.

There are some analogies to this concept in nature. Some types of pine can reproduce only if the forest burns. Under normal conditions, their cones stay shut, and the life-giving seeds cannot escape their resin prison and grow. Jesus pointed out that "unless a kernel of wheat falls to the ground and dies, it remains a single seed. But if it dies, it produces many seeds" (John 12:24). When our bodies are forming in the womb, all sorts of tissues grow only to die immediately, like the skin tissues that once existed between our fingers and toes and between our arms and our body. In order for us to grow and have freedom of movement, these tissues had to die even as our bodies were formed. Exercise is a form of breaking down our body tissues so they can grow stronger when they are rebuilt.

None of this is to say that fires do not cause immense damage or that improper exercise does not sometimes harm us more than it helps us. Rather, some sorts of growth come only in the face of opposition, adversity, and the breakdown even of what is good.

Our trust in the soul-making capacity of God is not that we will never suffer, nor that every suffering will immediately take on a meaning we can plainly see. Rather, it is that "a long obedience in the same direction"[1] will gradually shape us into Christlike people. We hope that conditions of suffering will not be entirely wasteful but that the extremity of involuntary suffering will reveal or form something of the greatness of the human spirit that otherwise would have remained hidden or unmade. Saints are not born; they are forged through adversity.

This is no justification for sitting idly by and watching suffering happen. This argument has nothing to do with the ethics of our response to suffering. Nor is it ever a sensible thing to say to someone, "This is all happening for your own good; think of all the growth that is coming from this suffering!" However, in our own hearts and lives, we can recognize the paths of freedom that have come through adversity. We can recognize this narrative even if it should never be imposed by another. Our witness of the good born out of pain in our own lives and in the lives of others may be a source of courage as we enter another bout of pain. It may help us see why God does not prevent all extremes of suffering, because the extremes of holiness are strangely and mysteriously linked to them.

You breathe deeply of the herb-scented air and turn to your boat once again. Where to next?

Let me hear more about God's attractiveness. (Turn to p. 83 [ch. 29].)

God makes meaning out of our lives. (Turn to p. 87 [ch. 30].)

God suffers with us. (Turn to p. 92 [ch. 31].)

I'm ready to move on from divine action. (Turn to p. 98 [ch. 33].)

1. This is the title of one of Eugene Peterson's excellent books. It is well worth a read.

CHAPTER 33

Individual Suffering

You are finished with the islands and make your way to the far side of the lake. You tie up your boat at the dock there. It is time to walk again. You set out with refreshed legs to follow the road.

You've just explored a few different ways God is at work in the world when we suffer. God is acting in the world to redeem suffering, to draw all creatures into loving relationship, and to build them into the kind of creatures who have the capacity to love.

From a bird's-eye view, the world and its suffering look small. From space, you see a beautiful marble of a planet, bursting with life—bright oceans, vibrant forests, and shining cities cover the face of the earth. From a distance, you don't see suffering.

Many of the "solutions" to the problem of suffering are kind of like that picture from space. They point to a "bigger picture" that makes our suffering look small, or at least necessary. "You can't have omelets without breaking some eggs" is wisdom that goes hand in hand with a "no pain, no gain" approach. You can always weave a narrative of good eventually, if you are far enough away from the one who is suffering.

Rube Goldberg was famous for his sketches of completely preposterous machines. He would take a very simple task and find a ridiculously complicated way to accomplish it. An example is the "self-operating napkin." A gentleman is shown sitting at a table, eating soup. As he (1) raises his spoon, it (2) pulls a string that (3) uses another spoon to (4) launch a cracker into the air. A waiting parrot (5) jumps for the cracker. The parrot taking off (6) upsets the weight of the seesaw it was standing on, which (7) tips a small bowl of sand into a bucket. The (8) increased weight of the bucket (9) pulls on a string that (10) sparks a lighter. The lighter (11) lights the fuse of a rocket. The rocket is attached to a scythe that (12) cuts another string. The cut string (13) releases the pendulum of a clock that has a napkin attached to the bottom. When the pendulum swings over, the napkin (14) wipes the gentleman's mouth. As the entire contraption is attached to his head as a sort of elaborate headpiece, you can imagine the headache the gentleman must have!

Solutions to the problem of suffering also cause headaches. They take what seems to be clearly evil and unnecessary suffering and then add step after complicated step to try to build an argument to say that this is good after all.

"There was good in the death of the dinosaurs that they could not have foreseen," says the theologian.[1] "Their death opened up ecological spaces where mammals could flourish. As they developed, and grew more complicated, one particular species distinguished itself for its intelligence and group work. God took those animals and shaped them into the divine image: God taught them to love. God brought out the best in them: in rational thought, in creativity, in cooperation. Mozart and Bach touched the transcendent

1. This is my own argument paraphrased from passages in Bethany Sollereder, "The Purpose of Dinosaurs: Extinction and the Goodness of God," *The Christian Century* (September 23, 2013): 22–26, www.christiancentury.org/article/2013-09/purpose-dinosaurs; and Bethany Sollereder, *God, Evolution, and Animal Suffering: Theodicy without a Fall* (London: Routledge, 2019), 156–82.

glory of heaven in their music. All of this only happened because of the death of the dinosaurs. God redeemed the meaning of the life of a lost T-Rex in the moonlight sonatas, and the gentleness and beauty of love."

Step after step after step. Some theologians (not naming any names . . . do *not* refer to the footnote . . .) are not ashamed to build a Rube Goldberg machine that takes sixty-five million years to run! The point is this: suffering is easier to account for if you let yourself look beyond the immediate individual who is undergoing all the suffering. There is always some "greater good."

But those solutions fall away when a life is short or painful or both. If you focus only on the individual, a lot of suffering looks irredeemable. How is the goodness of God expressed to those whom death robs early in life? How is God good to those who never have a chance to flourish?

When you look squarely in the face of someone suffering needlessly, theology faces its sharpest challenge. How is God good to *this person* in *this situation*? There may be no earthly answer that satisfies.

Sometimes lives on earth end in brokenness. Sometimes the narrative arc of a story is tragic. Sometimes death steals before there is the chance to flourish. At these points, Christian theology often (and wisely) says there is no answer in this world that will satisfy. But there is another world.

Resurrection as a concept should not be turned to when all else has failed. It is not more powerful in hopeless cases. Instead, it is the proper end to every story, but our eyes are drawn more fully toward it when no earthly good can be found in an individual's life.

The road stretches before you, and as you follow, a flash of aquamarine on the horizon catches your eye. You walk on.

Continue your journey with redemption.

(Turn to p. 102 [ch. 34].)

CHAPTER 34

Heaven and Hell

Your road has brought you to the banks of the river of death. You thought it would be black and sluggish, like a river of tar. But you are surprised to find it sparkles, a clear green-blue color that reminds you of the Mediterranean Sea. It is a larger river than you imagined; the far banks are barely visible on the horizon—you simply gain the impression of a far green country. Spanning the river is the most magnificent bridge you have ever seen. It arcs like a perfect rainbow from this side to that. It seems to be suspended by magic; you can see nothing supporting it. You can't quite tell what it is made of, only that every time you look at it, it makes you feel warm and at peace. It is narrow. Only one can cross at a time, but you know at once that no one has ever fallen from it. You step out onto the bridge.

What is in store after death? Of course, we don't know. The classic Christian creed is "I believe in the resurrection of the body."[1] Today the word *resurrection* has been taken over by the vampire and zombie industry, so let's take a moment to review what it means.

---

1. A line found in the Apostles' Creed, originating from the early centuries of the church.

First, it means that we will have real, physical bodies, not that our spirits will live on in some cloudlike form. When Jesus was resurrected, he could eat fish and be touched. Other things were not the same: Jesus could appear and disappear instantly and was not immediately recognized by his disciples. Also, Jesus could not die again. In contrast to Jesus, Lazarus was brought back from the dead—he was revived or reinvigorated—but he was not resurrected. Lazarus had to face death again. A resurrected body never needs to go through death again.

The million-dollar question is this: What difference does Jesus make to those who die? Are all saved? Are only some saved? What happens to those who do not know Jesus? Every one of these questions has different answers depending on whom you ask.

Let's try a thought experiment to work out some options. Imagine God as a huge fire. (This conception is not totally unwarranted, as both Deut 4:24 and Heb 12:29 describe God as "a consuming fire.") Imagine people as one of five things: a dragon, a sick dragon, a rock, a leaf, or gold ore. When they die, people walk into the fire that is God.

A dragon in the fire is quite happy. That is their element. Indeed, everywhere else is a bit unsatisfyingly cool. The fire does not hurt or destroy the dragon. This is the picture of heaven: the redeemed soul in its element; the saint comes back to God.

Now imagine a sick dragon—in fact, a dragon with diseased scales. For this dragon, the fire is painful; the disease exposes the skin underneath to the fire that normally is not painful at all. Happily, the cure for the disease is simply to stay in the fire until the harmful bacteria are burned away. Then a new set of scales can grow, and the dragon can frolic in the fire with all her mates. This is somewhat equivalent to the idea that purgatory exists.

Encountering God will, at first, hurt like hell. But it will get better with time as the soul is purged of sin and turned into its proper self.

A rock is the third option. Now, we know that rocks aren't particularly feeling creatures, but the idea is to think of something that won't be destroyed by fire. A nice piece of granite could last forever in a fireplace. If the rock happened to be a sensitive rock, it would find that fireplace to be an uncomfortable place, but it wouldn't wear out. It would just go on being uncomfortable, unless it found a way out.

The leaf, assuming it is *just* a leaf, has already been cut off from the tree, bush, or vine from whence it came. (I always wanted to use *whence* in a book!) By the time we are holding it in our hand, it is already dead. Throwing it into the fire will not *harm* it further. The fire will simply consume what is left—take it out of existence entirely.

The last option is gold ore. Smelting is the process of heating an ore to extract a base metal, in our case, gold. Insofar as heat is applied, it is solely for the sake of revealing the gold inside every single piece of ore. Unlike for the sick dragon, this process is not uncomfortable for the gold; it is becoming what it was meant to be. This is roughly equivalent to universalism: the good in everyone will be revealed and saved. No one is entirely without gold, and God will find it in every case.

After you cross the bridge, five paths lie before you.

The path of the dragons and the rock: popular imagery of heaven and hell really do exist. (Turn to p. 115 [ch. 38].)

The path of the leaf: evil is destroyed entirely. (Turn to p. 120 [ch. 40].)

The path of the sick dragon: we need some healing before heaven. (Turn to p. 118 [ch. 39].)

The path of the gold ore: all are saved, so only heaven exists. (Turn to p. 122 [ch. 41].)

All these are only human choices! What about animals? (Turn to p. 106 [ch. 35].)

CHAPTER 35

Animal Salvation

You wander along the north road and into a most magnificent forest. It seems to be every kind of forest at once: jungle, pine, deciduous. It is not as if it is a little of all of them, or that it is rapidly changing from one to the other, but rather that it is seamlessly all of them at once. And it is full of life. Every variety of bird and mammal and lizard and insect surrounds you, but without stinging or killing or pouncing. You walk in wonder.

"Will my dog/cat/horse/hamster/aardvark be in heaven?" This is a common question, but one people often feel silly asking. I think it is perfectly reasonable to ask. As it turns out, it has been asked by many thoughtful people throughout the centuries. They have come up with several different solutions. People often think the debate over animals in heaven is a question about whether animals have souls. This is a slight misunderstanding. Animals were always thought to have souls. The debate was over whether they have the *kind of souls* that survive death.

As with so many debates in theology, the argument traces its roots down to Aristotle. Aristotle thought there were three kinds of souls: vegetative, sensitive, and rational. You didn't have just one;

you could have all three, like a pyramid with each part built on another. Humans have all three layers. Animals have the bottom two layers. Plants have the bottom layer only.

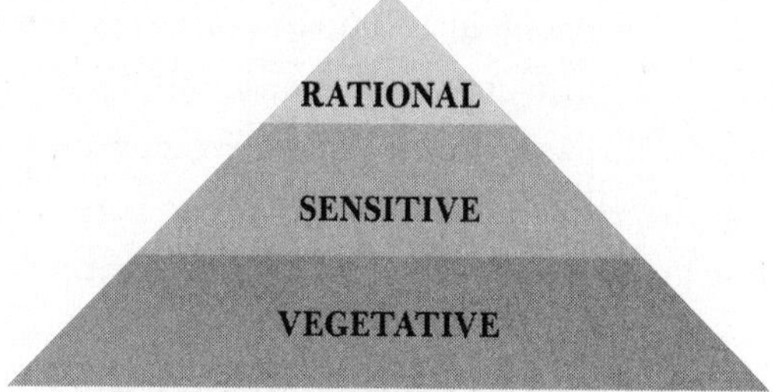

Each type of soul gives different capabilities to the creatures that have it. The vegetative soul allows one to grow and reproduce; it grants the basic features of being alive. The sensitive or animal soul allows creatures to move around and to sense the environment around them. Any animal that can see, taste, touch, smell, hear, and move has a sensitive soul (the ancients did not realize that plants do many of these things, just differently). Finally, the rational soul allows a creature to think, reflect, and act rationally. For Aristotle, this meant only humans have a rational soul. Since humans can grow, reproduce, move about, and sense the world, they also have vegetative and sensitive souls.

Do animals go to heaven? The first choice is with Aristotle and those who followed him, who thought that since you need a body to grow and sense the world, the vegetative and sensitive souls could not survive after the death of the body. Pure thought, or the rational soul, could endure the death of the body. The rational soul made life after death possible for humans but not for animals or plants. So, for much of the tradition, there was no life after death for animals or plants. This wasn't because they were not deemed important but because after their bodies died, there would be no surviving soul left over to go to an afterlife.

The second option is that only humans have the *normal* ability to survive death, but nonhuman animals can be granted that ability under special circumstances. C. S. Lewis and John Polkinghorne have speculated that animals with special relationships to humans, like pets, can be given eternal life. They can be personified by contact with humans and be included as part of the community of those who believe.

Finally, there is the view that animals *do* have what it takes to last beyond death. Whether that is because they have a soul that will endure death or because God will remember and re-create them, they are going to be resurrected in their own right.

If animals can be raised to new life, the question becomes, "How many?" Will there be just a few of each kind of animal with representation in the new creation, like a new Noah's ark of everlasting life? Perhaps there will be a cutoff line, similar to a height restriction at a theme park: "You have to be this intelligent to enter." Or will there be a great congregation of every creature that ever lived—all creatures great and small, from the mighty blue whale to the microscopic amoeba? Perhaps the right question to ask when it comes to redemption is, "What does God love?" If God loves worms and bacteria, then there is no reason they should be excluded from sitting next to the rabbit or the horse or the human in the new creation.

You come to a crossroads called "Fate of Other Life." Which way will you take?

Follow Aristotle: Other life doesn't have what it takes to survive death. (Turn to p. 110 [ch. 36].)

Follow C. S. Lewis: Some animals are redeemed through humans. (Turn to p. 112 [ch. 37].)

Follow the last path: Other creatures have souls that can survive death. All of them! (Turn to p. 122 [ch. 41].)

CHAPTER 36

Animal Souls Cannot Survive Death

You have chosen to follow Aristotle's path, positing that animal souls cannot survive death. The new creation will not include the same animals that have populated this earth. Perhaps God will create some new form of animals for human comfort and companionship, or perhaps the need for ecological wholeness will have passed away. Either way, only humans will wake up on the far side of death.

What does that mean for the purpose of animal lives? Is being eternal the only path to a meaningful life? What should we do with lives that emerge briefly, shimmer for a short while, and then disappear beneath the sands of time?

First, we could say, "Yep, they are totally meaningless." They were a stepping-stone in life's history, no more. God uses animals for human development and benefit, but once that is accomplished, they will disappear from the earth and have no more meaning. We should just get back to human redemption.

Second, we could look for the meaning of animal lives in the streams of lives that benefited from them. Nature never wastes anything or anyone; rather, every creature that dies is eaten, transformed, and carried on in other lives. Animals are redeemed through their ecologies, by feeding and supporting every other form of life. Redemption for an animal is entirely a this-world kind of thing.

Third, we could say that animals are remembered by God. God's memory is like the ultimate Hall of Fame. Every creature that ever lived is known, remembered, and treasured by God. The meaning of creatures that have long since departed, like the dinosaurs, still has a place in eternity because God knew them. Their lives are no longer experienced as an "I"; they have no personal experience of new life. But they do still exist in a sense by living on in the life of God. The meaning of their life is created by God and understood by God. They are remembered by God, and this gives them a kind of immortality because they have contributed to God's life. They won't have any personal experience of the afterlife, but their very existence contributed to ultimate reality in a way that brings God joy. In this case, the only meaningful thing to do is to return to human redemption, to those who might have the chance of continuing into the afterlife.

The path ahead forks sharply. One takes you back to human redemption; the other is the path to ecological redemption.

Take me back to human redemption.
(Turn to p. 102 [ch. 34].)

Animals are redeemed through their ecologies.
(Turn to p. 59 [ch. 21].)

Limited Animal New Creation

Your path leads you down a narrow lane. At the end is a flower garden near a large brick house with white trim around the many windows and a dark green door. As you approach it, the door opens, and an old Englishman greets you. He ushers you down a narrow hall and into a book-lined study that looks out onto the garden. As you sink into one of the large, deep armchairs, he leaves to get some tea. You breathe in the smell of tobacco and book dust and take a moment to reflect.

There are three possibilities for how and why animals might be included in the new creation if they are not innately able to receive eternal life.

The first possibility is that they are loved into reality. Have you read Margery Williams's masterpiece, *The Velveteen Rabbit*? It is about a stuffed toy rabbit who is loved by a nursery child. The toy rabbit meets some real rabbits one day when it is left out on the lawn. The toy rabbit is extremely jealous of their long legs and their ability to hop about rather than having to be moved by others. Another nursery toy, the old and wise Skin Horse, tells the toy rabbit that if he is loved sufficiently he will someday become a real rabbit. Years later, after the toy has long since been loved into a shabby state and finally forgotten by the now grown child, a fairy comes and turns the toy rabbit into a real rabbit. It goes out and joins the real rabbits in the woods.

C. S. Lewis and John Polkinghorne have a view of animal salvation that is kind of like the Velveteen Rabbit. Animals who are loved by humans are given a special pass into the afterlife, either because they are necessary to the happiness of the people or because they have somehow been made into persons because of their relationship with a human.

The problem with this view is that it seems a bit hard on creatures who never had a chance to know humans or creatures who are not generally loved by humans. The new creation, in this view, will have a lot of dogs but not many dinosaurs. Deep-sea squid will not be around, and there probably won't be many arachnids. (Although, my brother had a pet scorpion, so who knows?) It ultimately results in a rather human-shaped heaven.

The second possibility is that a few creatures of each species might be included so that every kind of animal has a representative, but the new creation would not include every creature that ever lived. Two or three of each kind of beetle is plenty. The fullness of the earth will be saved, but many individual creatures will live only in the memory of the God who loved them. The possible problem is whether we can be satisfied with just any representative. Will two representative dogs be good enough to represent the hundreds of varieties? We also might want more than just two. A herd of two zebras is not nearly as majestic as a herd of hundreds. And would all horse lovers have to share just the two horses?

The third option is that every animal needed for human happiness will be included. The Velveteen Rabbit approach requires animals to be already loved in order to make it. This third approach says that all the creatures who *one day might* add to our happiness will be included. If you've never had a horse, a horse will be there. If you have an undiscovered love for hagfish, they will be there for you to find. If eternal rolling grasslands are not complete without giraffes strolling across them, giraffes will be included. Humans are not at their best on their own; they need other creatures. The variety and beauty of the nonhuman animal kingdom will be preserved for human well-being.

In each of these scenarios, heaven is a place for humans. If other creatures happen to make it, so much the better for them. But they are not the main event. Animals in heaven are only a footnote to the story of God and humanity.

The old scholar returns with the tea. He hands you a cup, and you settle down for a good, long talk.

You have come to the end of this path.

Return to human redemption by turning back to p. 102 [ch. 34].

CHAPTER 38

Heaven and Hell Both Exist

As you walk along, you see a city in the distance, glinting gold under the sun. The sight of it fills your heart with longing. But your path does not lead there, at least not yet. It curves down, away from the city and toward a valley obscured by shadow.

Heaven and hell both exist. When we die, our lives will usher us forth into an afterlife destiny of either great joy or great pain—or maybe both.

People nowadays think that the notion of hell is barbaric, that an angry God sends you there against your will as a torment for having too much fun and not spending enough time telling God what a great guy he is. But hell is not about a divine hatred of pleasure. It is about justice.

We've all seen or heard about evil acts. I don't need to rehearse them here. Some of the people who commit these acts are caught and prosecuted by police. Many are not. The concept of heaven and hell means that people who genuinely did good in the world (and that often comes at one's own expense) will be rewarded for the good they did, and people who deserved punishment for the suffering they caused others will get what is coming to them.

Where heaven and hell get tricky, of course, is deciding who goes where. How much good must one have done to make it to the "good place"?[1] How do you decide if someone should go to the "bad place"? Some people think there is a massive points tally, and at the end of a person's life, they see how much good or bad they have done. If you are good enough, you go to heaven. Not good enough, and maybe you get reincarnated as a cockroach and have another go at trying to be good, this time with the less morally weighted choices of an insect.

Christians have generally thought that you only get one chance at life. We are born, we live, and we die. After that comes the judgment. The catch, in Christianity, is that no one is good enough to make it to heaven. Everyone has been smeared with sin. Even if we ourselves have not intentionally done wrong, we can be caught up in systems of wrongdoing—one big human spiderweb of sin that ensnares all of us.

How does that work? Well, imagine your friend has a baby. You own no sheep or cotton fields and don't know how to make cloth or weave. But you want to get your friend's new baby a onesie. So you go to the store, pick out a perfect little outfit that says, "Spit happens," wrap it in some tissue paper, and head to the baby shower. Perfect, right?

But then you start calculating: Who made that garment? Did they have good working conditions? Were they fairly paid? Where did the cotton come from, and how far did it travel from field to factory to store—in short, how much carbon did it use as it moved its way across the world? Does the store you bought it from offer proper wages and benefits to its staff? Or have they cut those back in order to make your cute little onesie that tiny bit cheaper in order to compete with the other store in the mall?

1. If you have not seen the TV show *The Good Place*, go watch it now. All four seasons. I'll wait for you.

As it turns out, in trying to get your friend a nice gift, you ended up participating in the exploitation of factory and field workers across the world, contributed to global warming, and justified the poor wages and lack of benefits for the people in the shop. We did not make the choices that created those injustices, but every day we make the choices that perpetuate them. No one is left out.

Some of us commit big moral atrocities. Others of us keep it small, telling just a little lie here or there, stealing only what no one would miss. But even without crime on the table, there are still a thousand ways to hurt one another and ourselves. In Christianity's view, everyone has made the wrong choices, done the wrong things. Which is why—thank God!—it is not our moral tally that counts. We are given the chance to take Jesus's tally instead of our own. Somehow, in the life, death, and resurrection of Jesus, we are given the possibility of being judged by Jesus's score sheet. His perfect point tally is offered to everyone.

Now just one choice remains. Some people might refuse that offer, so what happens to them? Do they stay in hell, its doors locked from within? Or is there a possibility that people can leave hell—that they can make better choices on the far side of death? Maybe it is never too late for redemption and to turn toward the path that leads back to the God of love.

A set of grey buildings fills the valley before you. Will you go in?

Hell is eternal. You can choose to end your path here.

Or learn more about the possibility of leaving hell and about the idea of purgatory. (Turn to p. 118 [ch. 39].)

CHAPTER 39

The Grey Town

You enter the valley, feeling a growing sense of dismay that you are leaving the golden city far behind you.

C. S. Lewis's *The Great Divorce* imagines both heaven and hell as eternal places, but no one is imprisoned in one or granted limited access to the other. People can choose to move between the two as often as they will.

In the grey town, which is revealed to be hell, people can have anything they want simply by thinking of it. Palatial houses, food, wine, or any luxury they desire is theirs simply by imagining it. The only thing they cannot conjure up are other people. Yet as soon as they have built their ideal palace, something or someone messes it up, and they move out—slowly expanding the suburbs of hell to epic proportions. People can have anything but find that without love, nothing satisfies. Desire just grows and grows, and they keep trying to make more things to fill the gap in their souls.

Anyone, at any time, can get on a bus to heaven. What many find, however, is that heaven does not suit their tastes. The new creation is not about them; they cannot hold on to their old grudges or clutch their sense of self-importance. Everything about heaven is about the other, about humility, about love. Those who still insist on feeding their own egos inevitably choose to go back to hell where they can indulge themselves.

Yet for a few people in Lewis's novel, the trip to heaven has more benefit. They realize they must give up the way they have lived. They can let go and be made new. Rebirth is possible. Friends and relations meet them and try to persuade them to choose heaven. Every chance is given, every grace is extended. But the choice, ultimately, comes down to them. Will they choose to turn away from themselves and learn to love? God's unlimited love prevents God from forcing people to choose their own good.

Those who do choose rebirth over returning to hell find that the grey town was merely purgatory. It was a place where they suffered temporarily as they learned to walk toward the light. It was like taking a bath in very hot water to be cleansed from the filth of sin. How many will take this opportunity to turn to the good? Will everyone eventually be persuaded to turn to the good? (Forever is a very long time to demonstrate that self-centeredness is not a great solution.) Or will some people continue to fend off every attempt to get them to choose the good?

You look back toward the golden city. Will you turn and go back there?

People can and will choose to refuse God forever. Your path ends here.

Everyone will eventually choose heaven, leaving hell empty. (Turn to p. 122 [ch. 41].)

CHAPTER 40

Annihilationism

As you walk along the road, you see other pilgrims walking alongside you. You notice the sun becoming brighter, brighter than it has ever been. Some of the people around you seem to sharpen under the light: they become more solid, more substantial, more themselves than ever before. Others seem to fade under the light, becoming translucent and indistinct before becoming impossible to see at all. The sun bathes you in a warmth as comfortable as love as you walk toward a city with golden spires in the distance.

Evil must end. For all the love and forgiveness of God, you still need a time when God makes all things right. That means evil needs a definitive end. Evil's chapter must finish.

If hell is real, you believe it must be eliminated. For hell to be eternal would be to give evil an eternal existence: one last fortress of evil's presence. Once people make the choice of rejecting God finally, God will step in and destroy all evil. People don't suffer forever. Those who are saved will finally be released from the threat of tyranny and evil.

A different way to think of it is that evil simply ceases to be. Everything that exists right now exists because it has some link to God. If you destroy that link, you don't keep existing; you simply cease to be. Like the leaf analogy from the earlier chapter, if you cut the leaf off, it does not continue to live—it dies. Eventually it hardens, crumbles, and disappears. In the same way, those who reject God don't get to keep some fashion of life apart from God. They are not independent beings. When they say to God, "I want nothing of you," God allows them to cut their umbilical cord to life and existence. In the intense light of God, shadows don't hide; they simply disappear.

The unredeemed don't suffer in hell. They don't suffer at all. They simply cease to be. God's destruction of evil is no better and no worse than letting it fall into nonexistence.

The difficulty with this view comes when one of the people we love ends up in the "unredeemed" camp. Can heaven be heaven to us without them? Could we ever give up on someone we love? Yet this view of heaven makes it necessary that we should learn to enjoy eternity apart from that smile, those eyes. They are gone forever.

On the other hand, it means true freedom from evil is achieved. Those in heaven will finally be able to know that the fight against evil and every injustice and harm is over. There is no more fear because all evil has finally been eliminated. There is not even a small corner of the smallest dust particle where evil still reigns. Rather, the love of God will permeate every nanometer of the new creation, and everyone will live in and by love. There will be no hurt, want, or need. Loneliness will be unknown, and the experience of fulfillment will accompany every task and every relationship. They were the shadows, and now the world has emerged into the light. You arrive at the golden city, and you enter its gates.

You have arrived at the end of this path.

To learn about other views of heaven and hell, return to p. 102 [ch. 34].

CHAPTER 41

Universalism

Your path leads to a great golden city. Trees and rivers and gardens wind their way through it. As you look closer, you can even see a full mountain range running through the city, though you can't quite figure out how both the wildness and quietness of the high peaks meld so perfectly with the urban setting. Beauty is everywhere. Everywhere you look is not just a sight but a vista. Even better than the architecture or the environment are the people. Everyone you loved in one place. Everyone you hated there, too, yet transformed now into someone beautiful and dear. Peace and joy wrap themselves around you, and over everything is love, calling you forward into greater adventures.

God's love never fails. God's love never loses, not in the end. Every creature God created and every person God loved will be saved—not by force or coercion but by faithful, gentle love. Animals and other life-forms that have no ability to choose will be included in the new creative work of God automatically. Humans will have free choice, but all will be given the time and the ability to understand the grace of God. They can reject God for as long as they like, but God will never give up until all are safely home.

"And I," said Jesus, "when I am lifted up from the earth, will draw all people to myself" (John 12:32). Not "the predestined." Not "the elect." But "all people."

Paul also gives intimations that Jesus's work was not limited to a few people: "For God was pleased to have all his fullness dwell in [Jesus], and through him to reconcile to himself all things, whether things on earth or things in heaven, by making peace through his blood, shed on the cross" (Col 1:19–20). Not "some things," but "all things" will be reconciled to Christ. That is the true power of God revealed in gentle, persuasive beauty.

No evil will go unredeemed. No broken relationship will remain fractured. All the tragic reality that surrounds us will be re-created into glorious new life. Instead of destroying what has been ruined by evil, God upcycles it. God transforms the ugly into something with new beauty. Nothing is worthless or discarded.

There are times when human sight fails to see value. We look at evil people, and we think that even hell might be too good for them. Why should they get into heaven alongside those who suffered for the sake of good? Did they just "get away" with all their evil? It is true that a universalist position has a sort of generous unfairness about it.

Jesus tells a story about a landowner who hires itinerant laborers to work in his vineyard (see Matt 20:1–16). Early in the morning, just as the sun is rising, he hires a round of people. Later in the day, he sees other men standing around, waiting for work, and he hires them too. Late in the day, just when the sun is about to set, he recruits a last set of men who work only one hour out of twelve. The vineyard owner lines them up and gives everyone the same wages: a full day's worth of money. The early morning crew is furious; shouldn't they get more than all the rest? But the landowner points out that they were given what they agreed to work for: a full day's wages. Why should they be unhappy that he is generous to those who could not find work earlier in the day?

In a similar way, God gives everyone eternal life. You can't give more eternal life or less eternal life. It is without measure. Nor can you give a better quality of paradise to some and give a second-class heaven to others, because heaven is made of God's love. It comes undiluted to everyone, and everyone will be equally transformed by it. Why worry, when growth will be measured in light-years, whether one person was a foot taller than another to start with? Such comparisons will soon be meaningless and forgotten.

Everyone will be transformed. No pain will be left unhealed. No longings will be unfulfilled. No relationship will be less than perfect. The ages of disappointment and pain and separation will be over. Everyone will shine through as themselves—more gloriously themselves than we could ever imagine. Joy and peace and plenty will be the rule.

If that is the vision God has, why didn't God just make that first? Why bother with this vale of tears?

There is no certainty in any answer that is on offer, but let's speculate a bit. Perhaps it is because heaven is not a place that can populate itself. Maybe we needed the earth to produce all the variety of people and penguins, seals and seagulls that could fill heaven. With all the varied Christian images of heaven, having babies is one thing that is not usually imagined in the afterlife. Perhaps reproduction is essentially time-bound. Once creatures are made, they can inhabit heaven. But there is no shortcut to making them in the first place.

In the end, we don't know the reasons God created the earth or allowed so much suffering. But our trust is in the Love that redeems, the Light that pierces every darkness, the Life that resurrects all dead. That Love and Light and Life will not allow a single person to perish, but rather, as Julian of Norwich wrote, "But all shall be well, and all shall be well, and all manner of things shall be well."[1]

You have come to the end of this path.

To learn about other understandings of heaven and hell, return to p. 102 [ch. 34].

1. Julian of Norwich, *Revelations of Divine Love*, trans. Barry Windeatt (Oxford: Oxford University Press, 2015), 74.

Afterword

Although I spent many happy hours as a child reading *Choose Your Own Adventure* books, the idea for this book did not come originally from them, or from the spate of Netflix movies that allow you to choose your own path through a plot. Instead, the heart of this book is in the science of the psychology of pain and in the difficulties that I encountered reading through many of the books that have been written about suffering and pain.

The first puzzle piece in creating this book came while I sat in wonder through a lecture by professor Irene Tracey about the way that religious beliefs have an influence on how we sense pain.[1] She talked about her experiments in which she would give volunteers a painful stimulus (this is scientist-speak for "electrocute them") and have them think about either a religious portrait or a secular one. As it turns out, even that very simple act of looking at a painting could change how much pain people felt. In particular, the devout Christians looking at a portrait of a biblical figure (in this case, the Virgin Mary) felt less pain than their atheist counterparts.[2] The

1. Fortunately, the lecture was recorded and can be found on the Faraday Institute website. Search for "Imaging Belief States in Pain and Religion," which was recorded on 27 November 2015.

2. Katja Wiech, Miguel Farias, Guy Kahane, Nicholas Shackel, Wiebke Tiede, and Irene Tracey, "An fMRI Study Measuring Analgesia Enhanced by Religion as a Belief System," *Pain* 139 (2008): 467–76.

scientists who ran the test conjectured that the anaesthetic effect was because the picture made them think about her life and her suffering, and it gave them more resilience in their own situation of pain. It changed the way they were thinking.

That process of changing the way we think is called *reappraisal.* There are several methods of psychological treatment that rely on reappraisal to do the heavy lifting in therapy. Cognitive Behavioral Therapy (or CBT) is one of those. The entire approach is based on the premise that the way you feel emotionally about a situation depends on how you think about it. For example, if you bring "all or nothing" thinking to every decision you make, you will be exhausted by the end of the day because every choice will be a big, heavy decision that threatens to overwhelm you. "All or nothing" thinking tells you that one wrong decision could ruin you forever. But for most of us, most of the time, our decisions (like what to have for breakfast) will have only minor consequences. We can learn to relax and not catastrophize every thought by realizing that we are thinking in "all or nothing" ways and choosing to think differently. CBT trains people to see these thought distortions and helps them to live healthier and happier lives by changing the way they think. The change might be something small, like learning how not to be afraid of needles. Or it might be something big, like thinking differently about our relationships or our purpose in life. Either way, the goal of reappraisal is to help us feel less pain, less anxiety, and thereby to suffer less. A noble goal indeed.

The second puzzle piece fell into place when I sat down for a meal with Professor Jamie Aten. It was one of those meals that change your life. We sat for hours as he told me about his fascinating research. Professor Aten, who founded the Humanitarian Disaster Institute at Wheaton College, studies how people's view of God affects their resilience in suffering.[3] When a major disaster hits, like a hurricane or earthquake, do people who believe in a God who suffers with them respond better than people who think God is hurling disasters from heaven as a judgment on their sin? It turns out, they do.[4] The way we think about God changes how we think about the things that happen to us. All those seemingly abstract concepts I had learned in theology class about the nature and character of God had real life consequences for people. (I know, this should be obvious, but I am not the quickest tortoise in the creep.) I began to think. If we can teach people to think differently about God, perhaps we can help them encounter their suffering in better ways, ways that would lead them to suffer less. Maybe the terrified anxiety of someone who thinks God is punishing them for their sin with a devastating earthquake can be alleviated, and they can instead be comforted by God's love.

This desire to teach people better ways of thinking about theodicy and the problem of evil in order to help them suffer less led to my third puzzle piece. The third piece was my own experience of how different people found different and even opposite explanations for suffering helpful.

From one perspective, different solutions are obviously going to be helpful because people suffer for very different reasons. The person who has stubbed their toe in the dark quite rightly has a different explanation for their pain than the person who is abused by a loved one. The tendency for theologians, however, is to come up with one compelling story that is supposed to fit all the situations. "It all comes

3. Check out what he does at www.wheaton.edu/academics/academic-centers/humanitarian-disaster-institute/.

4. Jamie D. Aten, Michael Moore, Ryan M. Denney, Tania Bayne, Amy Stagg, Stacy Owens, Samantha Daniels, Stefanie Boswell, Jane Schenck, Jason Adams, and Charissa Jones, "God Images Following Hurricane Katrina in South Mississippi: An Exploratory Study," *Journal of Psychology and Theology* 36.4 (2008): 249–57.

down to freewill," says one. "It is because God wants to give you opportunity to grow," says another. "God cannot prevent evil," says a third. But these are too general to be useful to the nuance of our lives. How could I write a book that would be flexible enough to account for the different causes of suffering and for the different life experiences and perspectives of those who found themselves suffering?

The difference in life experiences is the other tricky part here. During my first major heartbreak, I remember getting really angry when people told me that "this was all according to God's plan." That just made me not want to serve or trust a God who would put me through such circumstances! How many more plans of suffering did God have prepared for me? I wanted no part in it. The idea of God's plan was no comfort to me, and I began to explore other options, like open theism, to make sense of what I saw. Yet, other faithful Christians whom I loved and respected *really did* find deep solace in the sense that nothing happened to them outside the active will of God. Trusting that God had a plan that would make sense of their suffering allowed them to surrender and to accept their suffering. It brought them relief and comfort in a way it did not bring me any comfort at all.

It is possible that my inability to accept God's plan is a result of my brokenness and stubbornness. It may be that my friends' inability to accept that uncertainty is part of how God made the world is a result of their brokenness. But as I look to the Bible, I see a whole variety of images of God: as father, as fortress, as lover, as mother, as shepherd, as friend, as helper. I think this variety is included because no one image can fully convey who God is. I also think the variety is because not everyone experiences these images in the same way. Take, for example, the idea of God as father. I was lucky enough to grow up with an excellent father, and so the image of God as father was always one of easy acceptance, warm love, and genuine interest in my life. Yet some of my friends had absent or abusive fathers, and they talk about how difficult it was to always hear that particular metaphor used of God. God was a fortress and a refuge for them, a stronghold in times of trouble. Yet to try and think of God as father only sent them into a theological tailspin. That is not the fault of the metaphor. Thinking of God as a good father is a useful image and has been central to Christianity since its beginning. But some people's experiences of abuse have made that metaphor almost useless; it taught them entirely the wrong things about God.

The same, I think, is true about the explanations we use about why there is suffering. Sometimes, even a very good explanation for suffering can cause more harm than good. Other explanations, though perhaps less ideal, can offer people a way out of their confusion—like the bottom rung of a ladder that helps them begin to climb out of a pit they've fallen into. People will have time to get on to better explanations later, but the important thing is for them to start a journey of thinking differently, to take a first step.

It was when these three ideas—these puzzle pieces—came together that I began to think about this book. How could I write something that would allow readers to take a journey of reappraisal? How could I help people think about their views of God in a similar way to how CBT investigates how people think? How could I give people the tools to evaluate different pictures of God while allowing flexibility for past experiences or theological sticking points? And, most importantly, how could I help people make meaning of the suffering they have gone through when I have no idea what they have encountered? While these questions churned around in my mind, a possible solution emerged: allow the reader to pick their own path through the theodicy landscape. This gives them agency. It allows them to choose their own level of challenge. It also allows people to engage with a sense of play or adventure, without invoking an "all or nothing" mindset about the theological issues at stake.

This last point may seem trivial. Some people think that serious questions should only be addressed with utmost seriousness. Certainly, that is true of most books about the problem of evil I had read. They would usually show their serious intent by recounting the worst evils that humans have inflicted upon one another. For some readers, this may have been helpful, because it showed them that the authors were not simply lost in metaphysical speculation but were at least trying to address real situations. For me, it had the opposite effect. During my doctorate, when I read many books on the problem of evil, I found myself emotionally overwhelmed by the stories; I found myself weeping at the horrific stories of evil. That left me totally unable to pay attention to what the author was saying about God or the world (it is not easy to read through tears). Day after day of spending hours reading those stories left me feeling traumatized every time I opened a new book. It was not until I came across Eleonore Stump's *Wandering in Darkness* that I saw a different way.[5] Her examples of suffering were gentle: a brother cannot share his beloved music with a tone-deaf sister; a mother gives her child a medicine meant to help her child, but the medicine ends up damaging her child instead. Not rape, or torture, or murder—just good intentions gone wrong or frustrated. The gentle, emotional tone of the book allowed me to engage with her arguments in a way that felt like flying after having trudged through a swamp of arguments for months.

I found out later that science backs this up: that when we experience intense emotions, our ability to think about complex issues diminishes to almost nothing.[6] The same is true if we have experi-

---

5. Eleonore Stump, *Wandering in Darkness: Narrative and the Problem of Suffering* (Oxford: Oxford University Press, 2010).

6. Hilary Ison, "Working with an Embodied and Systemic Approach to Trauma and Tragedy," in *Tragedies and Christian Congregations: The Practical Theology of Trauma*, ed. Megan Warner, Christopher Southgate, Carla A. Grosch-Miller and Hilary Ison (London: Routledge, 2020), 47–63.

enced trauma. It is why we "lose our heads" in arguments and why we can't just think our way by ourselves through complex trauma. The parts of our brain that deal with questions like "What is God like?" shut down when we are experiencing intense emotions.

Knowing about this research and knowing that what I wanted was for people to *think* differently about why there is suffering, I chose an extremely gentle approach in this book. Apart from one chapter, there are no descriptions of intense suffering, and that one has fair warning. There are, I hope, no issues that could trigger anyone throughout the rest of it. I used humor liberally. None of this was because I do not know about real-life suffering or I think it is a topic to be taken lightly but because talking about suffering explicitly would disable many readers from being able to think clearly about how they think of God.

The form of this book, then, is a result of my combining different types of psychological insights. Whether this was the right combination of insights to help people, or whether it will fail in its aim of helping people to suffer less through thinking better about God and the world remains to be seen. It is, in that sense, an experiment. My guess is that some people will really like it. Others will not like it at all or find the format confusing and frustrating. I am eager to find out if it will be a fresh new avenue for people to explore theology, or if it will become a cautionary tale in how not to help. In either case, I am looking forward to learning more about how to accompany others through suffering as we investigate the mysteries of God and this world.

BETHANY SOLLEREDER
22 April 2021
Regent's Park College, Oxford

Acknowledgments

There is a long line of people to thank.

I am extremely grateful to Jamie Aten, whose research on people's spiritual responses to disaster helped me create the methodology of "compassionate theodicy" that led to this "pick your own path" approach.

My thanks to the many, many people who looked over the initial map, including but not limited to Christopher Williams, Seth Hart, Camilo Andres Garzon, Max Wood, Eva Braunstein, Rebekah Wallace, George Klaeren, Emily Qureshi-Hurst, Christopher Bennett, Alister McGrath, Paul Fiddes, Christopher Southgate, the Leeds University philosophy seminar, and the Edinburgh science and religion seminar. For help with research and reading specific chapters or early versions of the manuscript, my thanks to Pete Jordan, Simon Hewitt, Karen Arychuk, Loren and Mary-Ruth Wilkinson, Dean Nelson, Hannah Williams, Sarah Williams, Susan Adkins, Kitty Willis, Rich Cummings, Joanna Collicut, Wesley Wildman, and Richard Dawkins. A special thank you goes to my first two readers: Haley Hodges Schmid and Molly Boot. They patiently listened as I read out each chapter in the literary-soaked atmosphere of Oxford's Eagle and Child and other favorite Oxford haunts (including The Kilns). Thank you to the C. S. Lewis Foundation and Regent's Park College, who have provided excellent places to live throughout the years of writing this book. I'm also so grateful for Haley Hodges Schmid's amazing poem that she wrote to help me honor my parents in the dedication.

A huge thank you to Susan Bridge, who acted as my literary agent. You are brilliant, and I would have been lost without you.

This book would not have been possible without two research projects, funded by the John Templeton Foundation, that gave me the time to research and write. The first was the University of St. Andrews Fellowships in Science & Religion (JTF Grant ID: 59023), and the second was the University of Edinburgh, God and the Book of Nature (JTF Grant ID: 61507). I am grateful as ever to the people at all the Templeton Foundations who have supported so much work in science and religion, as well as to John Perry, Sarah Lane Ritchie, and Mark Harris, who have managed these grants. I am grateful to Alister McGrath for writing the foreword and for supervising the project that gave me the time to write this book, and to Celia Deane-Drummond, who is supervising my current work.

I am grateful to Sarah Gombis, who convinced me to work with Zondervan. I am thankful for the broken table at the American Academy of Religion conference that allowed us to meet. Its brokenness first forged this publishing alliance. I am grateful to my first editor, Madison Trammel, and to Joshua Kessler who took over the project, and to Chris Beetham for his copyediting skills.

To my family, the Sollereder clan in Canada (too many to name, but you all know who you are!), and my "bubble" family here in Oxford—Pete, Andréa, Lucy, and Alice: thank you for keeping me sane through the lockdowns.

APPENDIX 1

The Flowchart

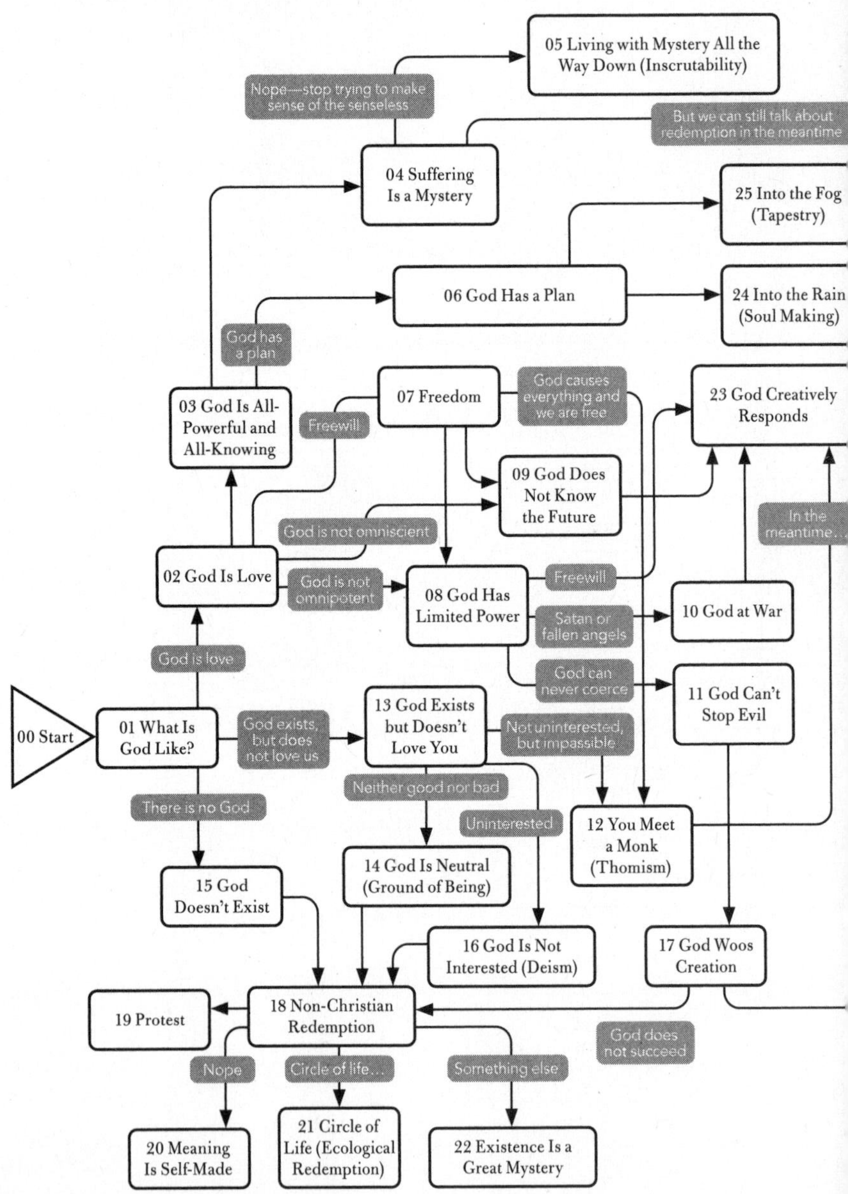

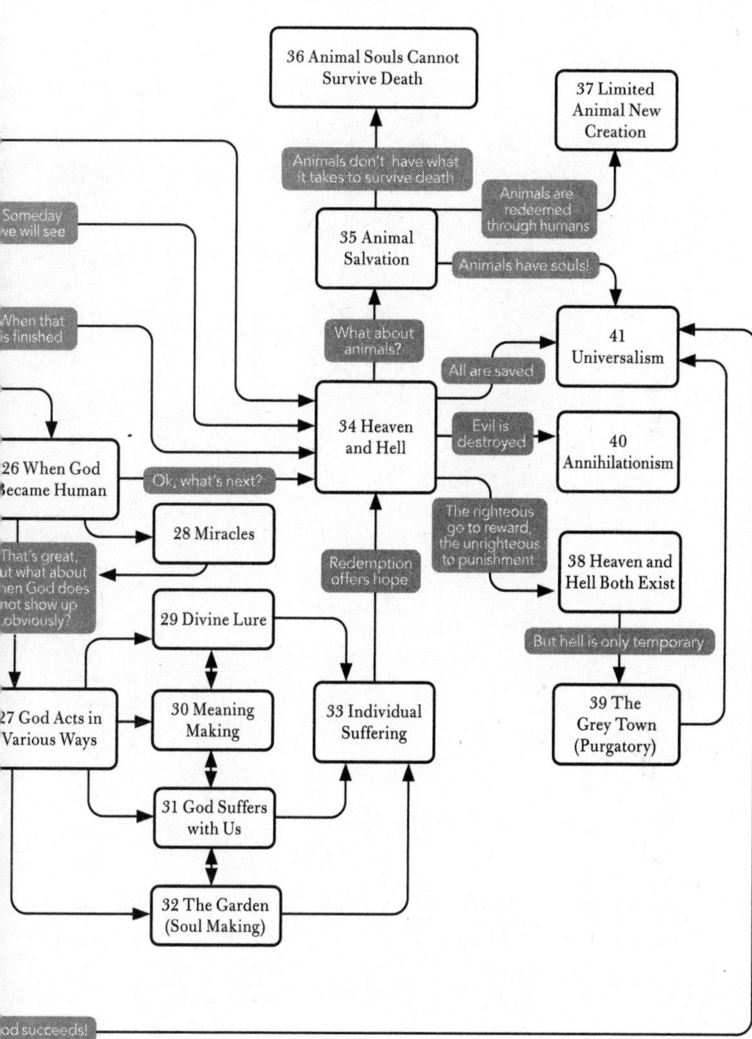
36 Animal Souls Cannot Survive Death
37 Limited Animal New Creation
Animals don't have what it takes to survive death
Animals are redeemed through humans
Someday we will see
35 Animal Salvation
Animals have souls!
When that is finished
What about animals?
41 Universalism
All are saved
34 Heaven and Hell
Evil is destroyed
40 Annihilationism
26 When God Became Human
Ok, what's next?
28 Miracles
The righteous go to reward, the unrighteous to punishment
38 Heaven and Hell Both Exist
Redemption offers hope
That's great, but what about when God does not show up obviously?
29 Divine Lure
But hell is only temporary
27 God Acts in Various Ways
30 Meaning Making
33 Individual Suffering
39 The Grey Town (Purgatory)
31 God Suffers with Us
32 The Garden (Soul Making)
God succeeds!

APPENDIX 2

The Map

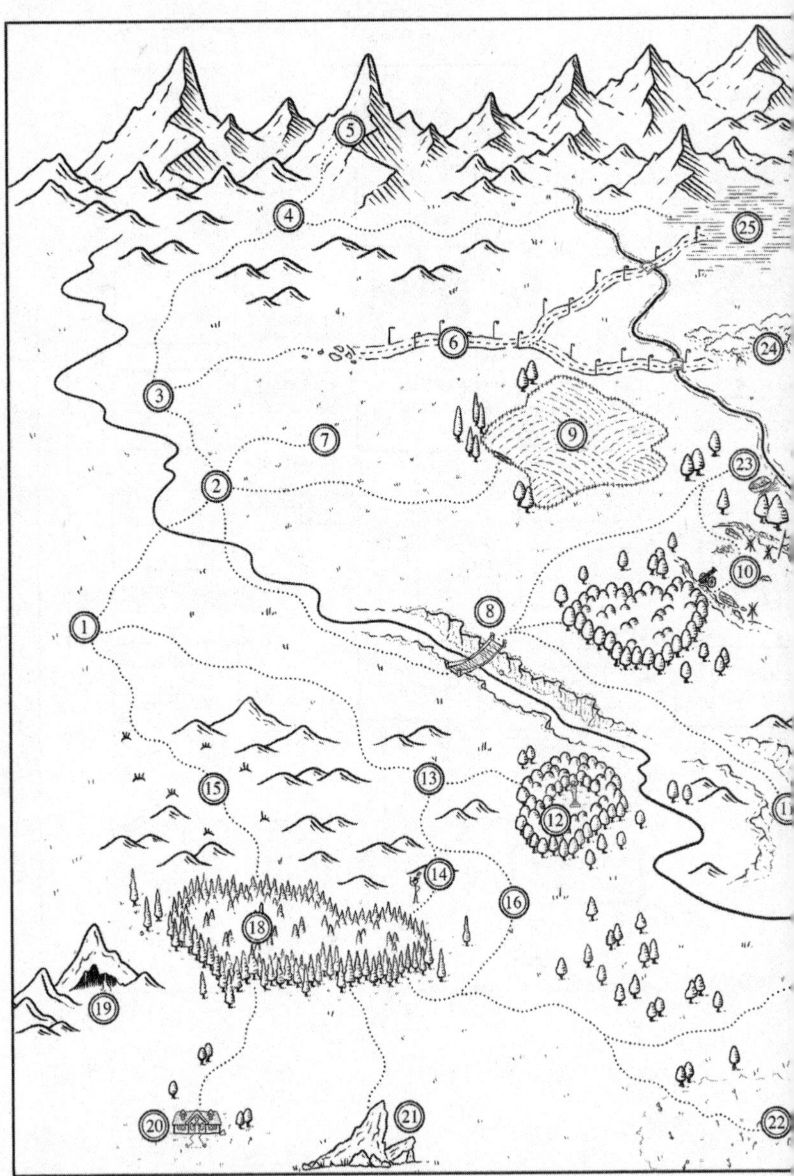

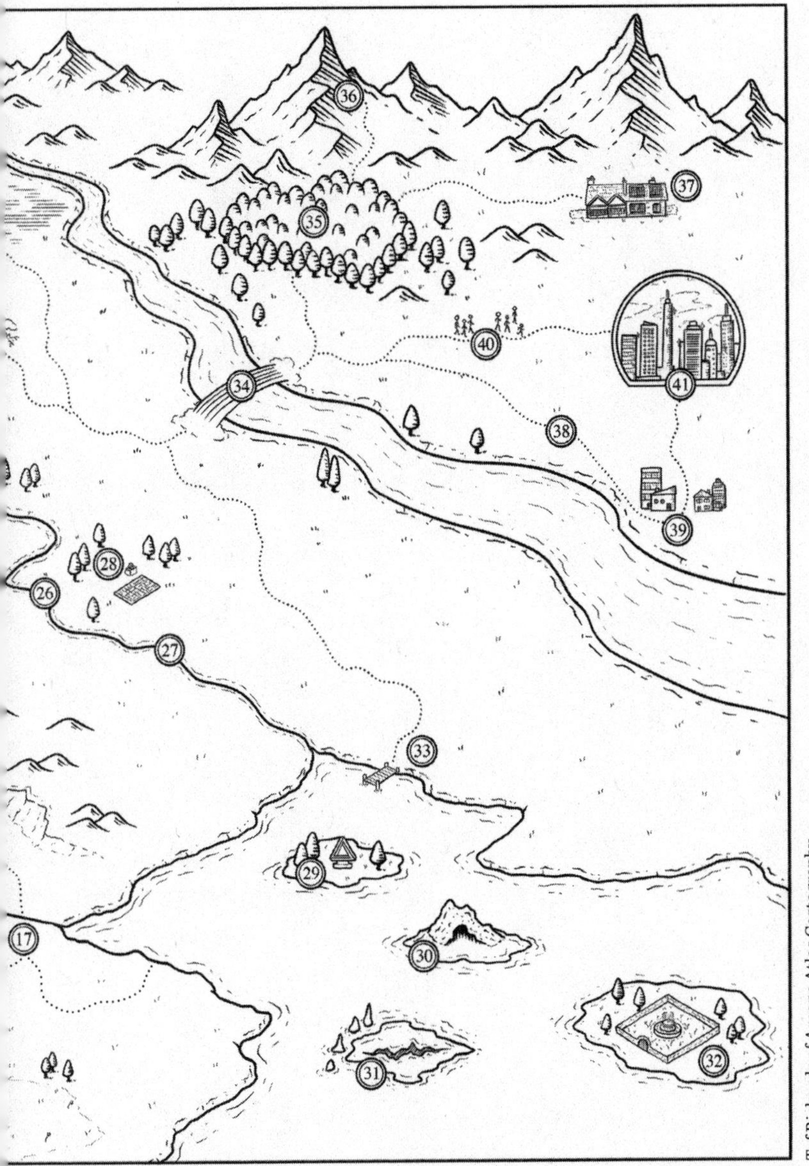

Taf Richards of Arcane Atlas Cartography

Bibliography

As opposed to most bibliographies, which are listed alphabetically by author's name, I have arranged these roughly in terms of accessibility. That is, the ones nearer the top of each section are easier to read, with the heavyweight academic texts nearer the bottom of each list. If you want to know more about a topic, try the top one. If you want to jump into a dissertation on the topic, try the bottom one. A few books show up a couple of times under different headings. Please take this as my glowing recommendation of that book. The more times it shows up, the more I think you should read it.

If you want to read more about theodicy as a discipline, or about the history and defenders of each of these positions, take a look at these reference books:

Reference Books

Mark S. M. Scott. *Pathways in Theodicy*. Minneapolis: Fortress, 2015.

Stephen T. Davis, ed. *Encountering Evil: Live Options in Theodicy*. Louisville: Westminster John Knox, 2001.

Michael L. Peterson, ed. *The Problem of Evil: Selected Readings*. Notre Dame: University of Notre Dame Press, 1992.

John Hick. *Evil and the God of Love*. 2nd ed. New York: Palgrave Macmillan, 2007.

Barry L. Whitney. *Theodicy: An Annotated Bibliography on the Problem of Evil, 1960–1990*. New York: Garland, 1993.

1. What Is God Like?

Chad Meister. *Evil: A Guide for the Perplexed*. New York: Continuum, 2012.

Mark S. M. Scott. *Pathways in Theodicy*. Minneapolis: Fortress, 2015.

Michael L. Peterson. *God and Evil: An Introduction to the Issues*. London: Routledge, 2018.

Richard Rice. *Suffering and the Search for Meaning: Contemporary Responses to the Problem of Pain*. Downers Grove, IL: IVP Academic, 2014.

2. God Is Love

W. H. Vanstone. *Love's Endeavour, Love's Expense: The Response of Being to the Love of God*. Rev. ed. London: Darton, Longman & Todd, 2007.

Robert Farrar Capon. *The Third Peacock: The Goodness of God and the Badness of the World*. New York: Doubleday, 1971.

3. God Is All-Powerful and All-Knowing

John Hick. *Evil and the God of Love*. 2nd ed. New York: Palgrave Macmillan, 2007.

David Polk. *God of Empowering Love: A History and Reconception of the Theodicy Conundrum*. Anoka, MN: Process Century, 2016.

4. Suffering Is a Mystery

Nicholas Wolterstorff. "On Grief, and Not Theologizing about It." *Christian Century*. January 10, 2019. www.christiancentury.org/article/first-person/grief-and-not-theologizing-about-it.

Karen Kilby. "Evil and the Limits of Theodicy." *New Blackfriars* 84.983 (January 2003): 13–29.

Michael Bergmann. "Skeptical Theism and Rowe's New Evidential Argument from Evil." *Nous* 35.2 (2001): 278–96.

William Alston. "Some (Temporarily) Final Thoughts on Evidential Arguments from Evil." Pages 320–21 in *The Evidential Argument from Evil*. Edited by Daniel Howard-Snyder. Bloomington, IN: Indiana University Press, 1996.

Daniel Howard-Snyder. "The Argument from Inscrutable Evil." Pages 286–310 in *The Evidential Argument from Evil*. Edited by Daniel Howard-Snyder. Bloomington, IN: Indiana University Press, 1996.

Karl Rahner. "Why Does God Allow Us to Suffer?" Part 15 in *Theological Investigations*, vol. 19. Translated by Edward Quinn. New York: Crossway, 1961.

5. Living with Mystery All the Way Down

C. S. Lewis. *A Grief Observed*. London: Faber and Faber, 1961.

Nicholas Wolterstorff. *Lament for a Son*. Grand Rapids: Eerdmans, 1996.

John Swinton. *Raging with Compassion: Pastoral Responses to the Problem of Evil*. Grand Rapids: Eerdmans, 2007.

Thomas G. Long. *What Shall We Say? Evil, Suffering, and the Crisis of Faith*. Grand Rapids: Eerdmans, 2011.

Philip Hefner. "The Problem of Evil: Picking Up the Pieces." *Dialogue* 25 (1986): 87–92.

6. God Has a Plan

J. I. Packer. "Seeing God in the Dark." Pages 294–99 in *Serving the People of God: Collected Shorter Writings of J. I. Packer*. Vol 2. Carlisle, UK: Paternoster, 2008.

David Basinger. "In What Sense Must God Be Omnibenevolent?" *International Journal for Philosophy of Religion* 14 (1983): 3–15.

Keith Yandell. "The Greater Good Defense." *Sophia* 13.3 (1974): 1–16.

H. Schuurman. "The Concept of a Strong Theodicy." *International Journal for Philosophy of Religion* 27 (1990): 63–85.

Mark S. M. Scott. *Pathways in Theodicy*. Minneapolis: Fortress, 2015. Pages 35–37.

John Hick. *Evil and the God of Love*. 2nd ed. New York: Palgrave Macmillan, 2007. Pages 117–26.

John Piper and Justin Taylor, eds. *Suffering and the Sovereignty of God*. Wheaton, IL: Crossway, 2007.

7. Freedom

John Martin Fischer, Robert Kane, Derk Pereboom, and Manuel Vargas. *Four Views on Free Will*. Malden, MA: Wiley-Blackwell, 2007.

Alvin Plantinga. *God, Freedom, and Evil*. New York: Harper & Row, 1974.

Robert Merrihew Adams. "Middle Knowledge and the Problem of Evil." *American Philosophical Quarterly* 14 (1977): 109–17.

8. God Has Limited Power

Thomas Jay Oord. *God Can't: How to Believe in God and Love after Tragedy, Abuse, and Other Evils*. Grasmere, ID: SacraSage, 2019.

Harold Kushner. *When Bad Things Happen to Good People*. New York: Schocken, 1981.

Alasdair MacIntyre. *Difficulties in Christian Belief*. London: SCM, 1959.

J. L. Mackie. "Evil and Omnipotence." *Mind* 64.254 (April 1955): 200–212.

9. God Does Not Know the Future

John Sanders. *The God Who Risks*. Downers Grove, IL: InterVarsity Press, 2007.

Clark H. Pinnock, Richard Rice, John Sanders, William Hasker, and David Basinger. *The Openness of God: A Biblical Challenge to the Traditional Understanding of God*. Downers Grove, IL: InterVarsity Press, 1994.

William Hasker. *The Triumph of God over Evil: Theodicy for a World of Suffering*. Downers Grove, IL: InterVarsity Press, 2008.

Clark Pinnock. "God Limits His Knowledge." Pages 141–62 in *Predestination and Free Will: Four Views of Divine Sovereignty and Human Freedom*. Edited by Randall Basinger and David Basinger. Downers Grove, IL: InterVarsity Press, 1986.

Brian Hebblethwaite. "Some Reflections on Predestination, Providence and Divine Foreknowledge." *Religious Studies* 15 (1979): 433–48.

10. God at War

Nicola Hoggard Creegan. *Animal Suffering and the Problem of Evil*. Oxford: Oxford University Press, 2013.

Gregory Boyd. *Satan and the Problem of Evil: Constructing a Trinitarian Warfare Theodicy*. Downers Grove, IL: IVP Academic, 2001.

David Bentley Hart. *The Doors of the Sea*. Grand Rapids: Eerdmans, 2005.

11. God Can't Stop Evil

David Polk. *God of Empowering Love: A History and Reconception of the Theodicy Conundrum*. Anoka, MN: Process Century, 2016.

Charles Hartshorne. *Omnipotence and Other Theological Mistakes.* Albany: State University of New York, 1984.

Bruce G. Epperly. *Process Theology: A Guide for the Perplexed.* New York: T&T Clark, 2011.

David R. Griffin, Joseph Deegan, and Dan Bryant. *How Are God and Evil Related?* Claremont, CA: Center for Process Studies, 1988.

David Ray Griffin. *God, Power, and Evil: A Process Theodicy.* 3rd ed. Philadelphia: Westminster, 2004.

C. Robert Mesle. *Process Theology: A Basic Introduction.* St. Louis: Chalice, 1993.

Paul Fiddes. "Process Theology." Pages 472–76 in *The Blackwell Encyclopedia of Modern Christian Thought.* Edited by Alister McGrath. Oxford: Blackwell, 1993.

12. You Meet a Monk

Herbert McCabe. *God Matters.* London: T&T Clark, 1987. Pages 25–39.

Brian Davies. *Thomas Aquinas on God and Evil.* Oxford: Oxford University Press, 2011. Chapter 10.

Herbert McCabe. *God and Evil in the Theology of St Thomas Aquinas.* Edited by Brian Davies. New York: Continuum, 2010.

Eleonore Stump. *Wandering in Darkness.* Oxford: Oxford University Press, 2012.

13. God Exists but Doesn't Love You

Wesley J. Wildman. "Incongruous Goodness, Perilous Beauty, Disconcerting Truth: Ultimate Reality and Suffering in Nature." Pages 267–94 in *Physics and Cosmology: Scientific Perspectives on the Problem of Natural Evil.* Vol. 1. Edited by Nancey Murphy,

Robert Russell, and William R. Stoeger. Vatican City and Berkeley, CA: Vatican Observatory Foundation, 2007.

14. God Is Neutral

Wesley J. Wildman. *God Is . . . : Meditations on the Mystery of Life, the Purity of Grace, the Bliss of Surrender, and the God beyond God.* Eugene, OR: Cascade, 2019.

Wesley J. Wildman. "Incongruous Goodness, Perilous Beauty, Disconcerting Truth: Ultimate Reality and Suffering in Nature." Pages 267–94 in *Physics and Cosmology: Scientific Perspectives on the Problem of Natural Evil.* Vol. 1. Edited by Nancey Murphy, Robert Russell, and William R. Stoeger. Vatican City and Berkeley, CA: Vatican Observatory Foundation, 2007.

Paul Tillich. *Systematic Theology.* 3 vols. Chicago: University of Chicago Press, 1951, 1957, 1963.

15. God Doesn't Exist

Alex Rosenberg. *The Atheist's Guide to Reality.* New York: W. W. Norton, 2012.

William Rowe. "The Problem of Evil and Some Varieties of Atheism." *American Philosophical Quarterly* 16.4 (Oct 1979): 335–41.

Sam Harris. *The Moral Landscape.* London: Transworld, 2010.

J. L. Mackie. "Evil and Omnipotence." *Mind* 64.254 (April 1955): 200–212.

16. God Is Not Interested

Daniel Castelo. *Theological Theodicy.* Eugene, OR: Cascade, 2012. Pages 33–37.

Matthew Tindal. *Christianity as Old as the Creation*. Public domain, 1730. Chapter 12.

John Toland. *Christianity Not Mysterious*. Public domain, 1696.

Charles Blount. *The Oracles of Reason*. Public domain, 1693.

17. God Woos Creation

Robert Farrar Capon. *The Third Peacock: The Goodness of God and the Badness of the World*. New York: Doubleday, 1971.

W. H. Vanstone. *The Stature of Waiting*. London: Darton, Longman & Todd, 1982.

Ruth Page. *God and the Web of Creation*. London: SCM, 1996.

18. Non-Christian Redemption

Sam Harris. *Waking Up: A Guide to Spirituality without Religion*. New York: Simon & Schuster, 2014.

Anthony Pinn. *Why, Lord? Suffering and Evil in Black Theology*. New York: Bloomsbury Academic, 1999.

19. Protest

Fyodor Dostoyevsky. "Rebellion." Book 5, chapter 4 in *The Brothers Karamazov*. Translated by Ignat Avsey. New York: Oxford University Press, 1994.

Ursula Le Guin. *The Ones Who Walk Away from Omelas: A Story*. New York: HarperCollins, 2017.

William James. "The Moral Philosopher and the Moral Life." *International Journal of Ethics* 1 (1891): 330–54.

20. Meaning Is Self-Made

David P. Barash. *Through a Glass Brightly*. Oxford: Oxford University Press, 2018. Pages 25–32.

Alex Rosenberg. *The Atheist's Guide to Reality*. New York: W. W. Norton, 2012. Pages 2–20.

21. Circle of Life

Ursula Goodenough. *The Sacred Depths of Nature*. Oxford: Oxford University Press, 1998.

Thomas Berry. *The Great Work: Our Way into the Future*. New York: Bell Tower, 1999.

Loyal D. Rue. *Religion Is Not about God: How Spiritual Traditions Nurture Our Biological Nature and What to Expect When They Fail*. New Brunswick, NJ: Rutgers University Press, 2004.

22. Existence Is a Great Mystery

Linda Mercadante. *Belief without Borders*. Oxford: Oxford University Press, 2014.

Ronald Dworkin. *Religion without God*. Cambridge: Harvard University Press, 2013.

Ravi V. Durvasula and D. V. Subba Rao. *Extremophiles: From Biology to Biotechnology*. Boca Raton, FL: CRC, 2019.

23. God Creatively Responds

W. H. Vanstone. *Love's Endeavour, Love's Expense: The Response of Being to the Love of God*. Rev. ed. London: Darton, Longman & Todd, 2007.

Denis Edwards. *How God Acts: Creation, Redemption, and Special Divine Action*. Minneapolis: Fortress, 2010.

Paul Fiddes. *The Creative Suffering of God*. Oxford: Clarendon, 1992.

24. Into the Rain

Sharon Dirckx. *Why?: Looking at God, Evil and Personal Suffering*. Nottingham: Inter-Varsity Press, 2013.

Sheldon Vanauken. *A Severe Mercy*. San Francisco: Harper & Row, 1977.

Timothy Keller. *Walking with God through Pain and Suffering*. New York: Penguin, 2013.

John Hick. *Evil and the God of Love*. 2nd ed. New York: Palgrave Macmillan, 2007. Pages 253–61.

25. Into the Fog

Robert Mackenzie. *The Loom of Providence*. New York: Fleming Revell, 1904.

Jean Pierre de Caussade. *Abandonment to Divine Providence*. Mineola, NY: Courier, 2014. Page 98.

Leslie Dixon Weatherhead. *Pain and Providence*. London: Epworth, 1935. Page 13.

26. When God Became Human

Paul Brand and Philip Yancey. *The Gift of Pain*. Grand Rapids: Zondervan, 1997.

Amy Orr-Ewing. *Where Is God in All the Suffering?* Epsom, UK: Good Book, 2020.

Jürgen Moltmann. *The Crucified God: The Cross of Christ as the Foundation and Criticism of Christian Theology*. Translated by R. A. Wilson and John Bowden. Minneapolis: Fortress, 1993.

Lewis S. Ford. "The Power of God and the Christ." *Religious Experience and Process Theology*. Edited by Harry James Cargas and Bernard Lee. New York: Paulist, 1976. Pages 79–92.

27. God Acts in Various Ways

Bethany N. Sollereder. *God, Evolution, and Animal Suffering: Theodicy without a Fall*. London: Routledge, 2019. Chapter 5.

George Mavrodes. "Is There Anything Which God Does Not Do?" *Christian Scholar's Review* 16 (1987): 383–93.

28. Miracles

David Hume. "Of Miracles." Section 10 in *An Enquiry concerning Human Understanding*. 1748.

C. S. Lewis. *Miracles*. London: Fontana, 1960.

Craig Keener. *Miracles: The Credibility of the New Testament Accounts*. 2 vols. Grand Rapids: Baker Academic, 2012.

29. Divine Lure

Robert Farrar Capon. *The Third Peacock: The Goodness of God and the Badness of the World*. New York: Doubleday, 1971.

Ruth Page. *God and the Web of Creation*. London: SCM, 1996.

Elie Pritz. *Peace Heroes*. Available online: https://globalpeaceheroes.org/.

David Griffin. "Philosophical Theology and Pastoral Ministry." *Encounter* 33 (1972): 230–44.

Bernard Loomer. "Two Conceptions of Power." *Process Studies* 6 (1976): 3–32.

Lewis Ford. *The Lure of God: A Biblical Background for Process Theism.* Philadelphia: Fortress, 1978.

30. Meaning Making

Kenneth Kramer. "The Daoist Farmer." Page 118 in *World Scriptures: An Introduction to Comparative Religions.* Mahwah, NJ: Paulist, 1986.

Marilyn McCord Adams. *Horrendous Evils and the Goodness of God.* Ithaca, NY: Cornell University Press, 1999.

31. God Suffers with Us

Robert Farrar Capon. *The Third Peacock: The Goodness of God and the Badness of the World.* New York: Doubleday, 1971.

Thomas Jay Oord. *The Uncontrolling Love of God: An Open and Relational Account of Providence.* Downers Grove, IL: IVP Academic, 2015.

Paul Thelakat. "God Suffers Evil." *Louvain Studies* 14 (1989): 16–25.

Paul Fiddes. *The Creative Suffering of God.* Oxford: Clarendon, 1992.

32. The Garden

John Hick. *Evil and the God of Love.* 2nd ed. New York: Palgrave Macmillan, 2007. Pages 253–61.

Richard Swinburne. *Providence and the Problem of Evil.* Oxford: Clarendon, 1998.

33. Individual Suffering

Eleonore Stump. *Wandering in Darkness.* Oxford: Oxford University Press, 2012.

Marilyn McCord Adams. *Horrendous Evils and the Goodness of God*. Ithaca, NY: Cornell University Press, 1999.

34. Heaven and Hell

Denny Burk, John G. Stackhouse, Robin A. Parry, and Jerry L. Walls. *Four Views on Hell*. Grand Rapids: Zondervan, 2016.

35. Animal Salvation

Jay McDaniel. *Of God and Pelicans: A Theology of Reverence for Life*. Louisville: Westminster John Knox, 1989.

Paul Griffiths. *Decreation: The Last Things of All Creatures*. Waco, TX: Baylor University Press, 2014.

Christopher Southgate. *The Groaning of Creation: God, Evolution, and the Problem of Evil*. Louisville: Westminster John Knox, 2008.

Trent Dougherty. *The Problem of Animal Pain*. New York: Palgrave Macmillan, 2014.

Bethany N. Sollereder. *God, Evolution, and Animal Suffering: Theodicy without a Fall*. London: Routledge, 2019.

36. Animal Souls Cannot Survive Death

See bibliography for chapter 20.

37. Limited Animal New Creation

John Polkinghorne. *The God of Hope and the End of the World*. London: SPCK, 2002. Pages 122–23.

Denis Alexander. *Creation or Evolution: Do We Have to Choose?* Oxford: Monarch, 2008. Pages 279–81.

38. Heaven and Hell Both Exist

Denny Burk, John G. Stackhouse, Robin A. Parry, and Jerry L. Walls. *Four Views on Hell.* Grand Rapids: Zondervan, 2016. Pages 17–60, 145–90.

Benjamin McCraw and Robert Arp, eds. *The Concept of Hell.* New York: Palgrave Macmillan, 2015.

Oliver Crisp. "Divine Retribution: A Defence." *Sophia* 42 (2003): 35–52.

39. The Grey Town

C. S. Lewis. *The Great Divorce.* London: Geoffrey Bles/Centenary, 1945.

Denny Burk, John G. Stackhouse, Robin A. Parry, and Jerry L. Walls. *Four Views on Hell.* Grand Rapids: Zondervan, 2016. Pages 145–90.

40. Annihilationism

Denny Burk, John G. Stackhouse, Robin A. Parry, and Jerry L. Walls. *Four Views on Hell.* Grand Rapids: Zondervan, 2016. Pages 61–100.

Edward Fudge. *The Fire That Consumes: A Biblical and Historical Study of the Doctrine of Final Punishment.* Houston: Providential, 1982.

41. Universalism

Rob Bell. *Love Wins.* London: Collins, 2012.

Gregory MacDonald. *The Evangelical Universalist.* Eugene, OR: Cascade, 2006.

Denny Burk, John G. Stackhouse, Robin A. Parry, and Jerry L. Walls. *Four Views on Hell*. Grand Rapids: Zondervan, 2016. Pages 101–44.

Thomas Talbott. *The Inescapable Love of God*. 2nd ed. Eugene, OR: Cascade, 2014.

Brad Jersak. *Her Gates Will Never Be Shut: Hope, Hell, and the New Jerusalem*. Eugene, OR: Wipf & Stock, 2005.

David Bentley Hart. *That All Shall Be Saved: Heaven, Hell, and Universal Salvation*. New Haven: Yale University Press, 2019.

Marjorie Suchocki. *The End of Evil: Process Eschatology in Historical Context*. Albany: State University of New York Press, 1988.

Contents